i

The Black Book

An Anthony Mann Reader

By Scout Tafoya

An Honors Zombie Book

Most times I think about the question of the greatest film artist who ever lived the answer comes to me easily: Orson Welles. He knew where the camera was meant to go, how it was meant to move, how you save a production that's losing money every second it continues, and how to confuse, confound, and stupefy an audience without ever losing them. When he desperately needed a hit, he made one. When he needed money he went out and got it. He would direct his own scenes in other people's movies, reasoning correctly that no one was going to do it better than he did. He never compromised. Never threw up the white flag. Never stopped hustling till the day he died.

I bring Welles up because he was an anomaly. He wasn't born to the world of film, he didn't come up as an assistant or a technician, he didn't force his own discovery, he was no one's son and heir. He was a talent on the stage, then the radio, and so yes, why not film? He fell into it like a child into a ballpit and produced masterpieces, though hardly any were recognized or without massive production problems. His narrative is mythic. The boy wonder who could never recapture the success of his first film, who never returned to the mediums that made him, who ended up doing commercials for bottom shelf wine while full to the brim with it to pay for some of the best and most distinct works of American art of all time. Telling the story of a much more conventional film artist presents a challenge, and I'll be honest, I couldn't look at the life of Anthony Mann and find a clever summation, a neat throughline, a story told in or by his art. He was not his lead characters, except possibly for the marked-for-death Eberlin in his final film, *A Dandy in Aspic*. The character might die twice and Mann died filming the movie.

Here is what I wrote for the intro of my Unloved, the video essay series I've written and edited for RogerEbert.com for the last ten years: After a career as a jobbing director of B-movie musicals, becoming one of the most important figures in the codification of American noir and the post-war Western, turning Jimmy Stewart from a romantic comedy lead into a hard bitten anti-hero, and finally cashing in his chips to become a maker of epics for Samuel

Bronston, friend of fascist Spain, Anthony Mann was a man out of his body. Twice divorced, in gambling debt, no longer working in his home country, and having traded in his ideals to make the hopeless *El Cid* as a favor to Generalissimo Francisco Franco, Mann had become the ultimate victim of capitalism. And for his last act, a lacerating self-investigation about a man trapped between countries and allegiances, who may, under all his subterfuge and deception, may just be the thing he despises most of all: a man. Himself.

And yes, that does cohere, after a fashion, and it's certainly compelling but the details don't add up to a story. They're a life, and a career, just like any man in post-war America might have enjoyed. The early pictures are impersonal but have the pizzaz and verve a young man would bring to such an occupation. The later movies are brilliant and *specific* but they no more tell you Mann's morals or ambitions beyond, once again, making something as cinematic as possible. Andrew Sarris puts it thusly in his book *The American Cinema,* which would help turn men like Mann from studio cogs into artists in the public consciousness. "His

Westerns are distinguished by some of the most brilliant photography of exteriors in the history of the American cinema, and yet it is impossible to detect a consistent thematic pattern in his work." Sarris nevertheless rewarded him with a spot in *Cinema's* "Far Side of Paradise" category; the runner-up file. Second best. Not too shabby.

Welles had only made four released films by the time Mann changed his playbook completely and became for a moment, the B-Movie stylist Welles wouldn't quite allow himself to be, whose love of upending detective stories and treating Shakespeare with a kind of pagan sincerity became his trademarks. Trademarks Mann would never quite develop. Though Fernando F. Croce, one of the best critics alive, countered with this in Slant Magazine a little over a decade ago: "Mann was an impeccable image-smith and a pitiless choreographer of brutality. Film noir was seldom blacker and the Old West never more severe than with him at the helm, yet his three-decade career displays a steely cinematic intelligence that transcends the facile "tough-guy" label his films were originally stuck with. Though it can be broken down into stages by genre, his is a remarkably consistent worldview of betrayal, pain, and the physical-spiritual toll of men obsessed with conquering nature and each other." He is, of course, not wrong, but bounding through his filmography at a gallop, as I did for this project, I had a hard time holding onto those consistencies. It was all *his,* but I can't say I could always form an image of who he was and what that meant...

Though it's got a different kind of theatricality, *The Black Book* or *Reign of Terror* would be a movie Welles would have been proud to make. Anyone would. With pennies to spend, he, cinematographer John Alton and production designer William Cameron Menzies, both on hot streaks, (all of them on their way to early retirement in their 60s, one by choice) created a kind of backlot hellscape a la Edgar Ulmer's *Detour,* but wilder, crazier, darker. This is a film set in the French Revolution made between film noirs and shot like one. The actors all but jump on each other, so intense are their performances and chemistry. After but a few seconds you forget about the "trying" part of "trying to make a costume picture on a budget" and give in to the achieving. It casts a spell as few other films do. And yet… Mann never became the artist you'd expect to emerge from such a hothouse fracas. Where was the romantic follow-up, the *Jane Eyre,* the *Wuthering Heights,* the *Chimes at Midnight,* as Welles would give us. Where was the modernist ambition?

It could be that Mann never quite developed any, though he was eventually rewarded with gargantuan budgets for his worst films. He was born Emil Anton Bundsmann in San Diego to an academic father and a drama teacher mother. Dad was from Bohemia, Mom from Macon, Georgia, and they were Theosophicals, an obscure and mostly forgotten new age religion. They moved to Austria to get Emile Sr. medical attention and left 3-year-old Emil in the care of the Lomaland Theosophical Society. When they came back their son was 14. They moved to New York and he became the star of high school plays, then a stage actor, production manager, a talent scout, a casting director, Preston Sturges' assistant director, the director of two shorts I cannot locate, and then made the leap to features (those shorts were made for an experimental NBC affiliate television station called W2XBS, founded in 1928, which made history when it ran the first *Felix The Cat* cartoon). The old story about the guy who started in the mailroom and retired as president of the company. Or he would have without the gambling habit and the ex-wives. The man whom Jacques Rivette would later call one of the four best post-war American directors worked as a nightwatchman at Westinghouse while he acted during the day. He rose through the ranks of the Theatre Guild and started directing shows but there wasn't enough room for Mann to grow. He moved to Hollywood in 1937, changed his name and, thanks to friends in high places, found himself behind the camera.

So, like Welles he came from theatre, had a couple of short subjects before his debut in the early 40s, and would later travel the world making (would-be) epics in desperate need of more money, marrying and divorcing a passel of women, and still to this day facing an uphill climb towards the pantheon. As I wrote in my Tobe Hooper book, the narrative of the boy genius who never reclaimed the highs of his first success is one of film land's favourites, and it is a tougher rap to beat than murder. But Mann's reputation was never anything in danger among serious cinephiles. French and American critics did, in their way, appreciate what he was up to, and today the Martin Scorseses and Wim Wenders of the world, directors who came of age while he was making films, gave him their praise and attention. Sarris, Jean-Luc Godard, and Robin Wood praised him when they were alive and writing, and closer to the present Jonathan Rosenbaum and my dear Dan Sallitt, some of our most serious critics in other words, have sung his praises quiet mellifluously. He is even the subject of a reverential aside in an early bit of Patton Oswalt stand-up!

Basically: There was no need for me to try and stretch this to the proper length of a book. No, this little volume is not the definitive study of Mann, nor is it something I poured quite the love and time into that I did *But God Made Him A Poet,* my book on John Ford or *Cinemaphagy* on Tobe Hooper. Those came from a need. Mann came to me out of a curiousity and a curiousity he remains. I studied him, I lived in his work, and I plan to vacation there again as often as I can, but I don't feel as though I found something in his works that cracks the code of Anthony Mann. His work adheres to a neat framework like the chapters of a book. First is the early experiments in style and light genre fare. Then the crime films, the noir, which bleed into the westerns with transitional works *The Furies, Devil's Doorway* and *The Tall Target*. He embraces widescreen in time to make the White Elephant art, the Americana and the roman epics, only broken up and then capped by the supremely dark pair *Men in War* and *A Dandy in Aspic*. Even that is a sloppy conditional reading of a career that lasted 26 years and 40 films.

There will be special emphasis placed on *The Black Book or Reign of Terror,* a film on which I'd considered pitching a BFI Classics monographs, but knew better than to pitch another book when I had the bulk of one on my hands already. Besides nothing tells you that you don't have the full material for a book like the fear of pitching it. I hate pitching just about as much as I hate rejection. Aside from the additional text on B*lack Book*, this is exactly what the people on my patreon read in the last year and change when I started writing about Mann, Clint Eastwood, Jacques Tourneur, Jaume Collett-Serra, and M. Night Shyamalan.

This is a work of pure appreciation of a man who figured out cinematic language, poured his every ounce of energy and ingenuity into his work, and then died most unbeloved by the film industry. He is a director whose failures and successes seem to keep each other in check, never allowing his greatness canonical status. Anthony Mann is a name every American cinephile learns, but we are not encouraged to make a spectacle of our love for him. So that's just what I'm doing. Here you'll find reviews of every extent Mann film on which he filmed more than B-Roll (so, blissfully, nothing on *Quo Vadis,* which spared me the indignity of having to watch it again) laced with personal anecdotes, tangents, and allusions. I have done my best to put Mann in context and out of it, to entice readers to go looking for meaning where perhaps I missed it. Without further ado:

Doctor Broadway – 1942

Anthony Mann began his career in bright lights. Neon signs flashing his name and the names of his cast and crew in Midtown Manhattan on marquees and stock tickers, portending great things for the one-time Paramount assistant director. Nothing but an inevitable rise would have done for *this* director. Mann used to claim different things about his past to different people. Peter Ustinov used to tell people the religious sect he'd grown up in. Philip Yordan said he grew up dirt poor. His father German catholic, his mother Jewish. He didn't have a real hit for the first decade of his career in Hollywood and even so he never became the kind of director stars request. He lived a workhorse and died one. By the time he made *Dr. Broadway* he was halfway to his death.

Dr. Broadway, real name Timothy Kane (Macdonald Carey who, like Mann, was just getting started) is a rake and a good

Samaritan in the same sturdy frame. First thing he does is talk a dame off a roof before she can jump and kill herself (Shane Black will steal this for his *Lethal Weapon* script) by acting crazier than she is and then knocks her unconscious before the police can arrest her so he can claim she's starving and that's why she jumped. He keeps drinking the booze they give her to come around. It's retrograde but it sings. *Moves* too, as when a woman wakes up in the back room of a mafia card game and she and the camera enter the space together, making sense of confusion just like that. The dialogue crackles, the camera drinks in the busy sets (in some instances sliding past them as if they were animated and no mass at all), lights flash on and off to mock desperation and draw out truths, actors practically dance with each other. This Anthony Mann fellow was going places.

Dr. Broadway is a *hair* nervous because he sent up mob flunky Vic Telli (Eduardo Ciannelli) a few years back with his testimony. He thinks Telli wants revenge but he really wants help. When he croaks in a couple of minutes he wants his money to go to his daughter (Joan Woodbury) who doesn't know he's a crook and he wants to keep it that way. He enlists Connie Madigan (Jean Phillips), the glory-hungry would-be suicide, as his new secretary in his search for Telli's daughter. He's got to hurry, too. Someone just killed Telli; his murder is filmed magnificently, as the opening of a door while Telli rests in welder's goggles in a chair. Truly uncanny stuff. Mann moves the camera around spaces in just the way Spielberg would later, never letting a change of dynamic interrupt a complete sentence. Like a movie drinking cup after cup of coffee and chain smoking. Mann wouldn't stay this guy but he could have and I wouldn't have complained, even if it means losing *Men in War*.

Moonlight in Havana – 1942

Anthony Mann's second feature isn't quite as brassy as his first but it didn't want for the same cockeyed ambition. Within the first 8 minutes we've seen six or seven impossible things. Allan Jones was a pitcher for a Baseball team currently losing their way to the bottom of the league standing ever since they suspended him. He goes to work as a cook and sings to pass the time in the kitchen. He sings so good that a talent agent hears him and offers him a gig singing in pre-revolution Cuba where the team that booted him are currently in spring training? Might he be able to, in less than this film's 59-minute run time, prove himself as a player and a crooner and win the heart of Jane Frazee in the process? Wouldn't *you* like to know?

Mann fares a little awkwardly filming the song and dance numbers knowing only that he has to capture the heads and feet of the performers during the choreography but taking too few chances beyond that. The dancers were all semi-established acts who get billed just after the main acting cast. There's some sub-Marx Bros farce (or maybe sub-Bowery Boys is more accurate) on board the boat south when the singing is done. Jones fakes sick to get out of his singing engagement so he can play ball again but it backfires. It's not a lot of plot, if you hadn't guessed, and none of it is particularly interesting. Mann compensates by trying to use the camera and edit to make a meal out of all this gruel but he's outgunned by incident. Almost exactly halfway through he starts to figure out how to shoot dance numbers (he cranes above a crowd of them and very briefly gets within stalking distance of off-peak Busby Berkeley).

There's some interest in the idea of Jones and Frazee singing to each other when they can't speak but it's insufficiently developed. As Jones ping pongs between his social cliques and careers Mann can do little but try and keep the camera trained on whoever's talking. The bald, doughy guys all start to blur together. Jones gets saved from having to pick between baseball and Broadway by a convenient thunderstorm (though Jones still has to hide in a fridge to shirk his responsibilities and fool a girl, predicting Indiana Jones). The film's brisk pace keeps it from developing an Ulmerian personality, for which the fake tropical location and pre-code plot surfeit could have allowed. Alas...this is every bit the thankless placeholder second step it appeared to me when I read the title.

Nobody's Darling – 1943

"He thinks he's Buzz Berkeley." Turns out I was onto something… This begins much more promisingly than did *Moonlight in Havana* and is itself something of a knowing joke about Mann's own career up until now, if not quite as cutting as if he'd been, say, Carl Laemmle Jr, a child of studio nepotism, but the crack about choreography seems very pointed. The film is about the children of stars at an exclusive boarding school. Mary Lee is the precocious daughter of Louis Calhern and Gladys George and as she sees what becomes of her mother's career, she preps her own by auditioning for a school play. The intro of the school is good, introducing us to a dozen distinct characters in about a minute, camera dollying across the X axis at lunch. George has been tossed out of Hollywood and her attempts to be a housewife yield a broken laundry press and a flooded kitchen. Calhern sympathy retires to humor George but that just makes her feel worse. As she crows melodramatically about going hungry both husband and daughter clap for her afterwards. Even in defeat they have to treat her like the diva she is.

There are excellent little jokes all the way through. Billy Dawson is a kid who wants to step into the shoes of a big shot, but when he lights a cigar to seem like a super producer it makes him sick, which pleases headmistress Lee Patrick to no end. She's been trying to wean him off cigarettes a little at a time. Mary Lee's huge feet keeping coming up in conversation; Jackie Moran rewrites the lead in the play to include how enormous they are. Lee is so put out by Moran initially not casting her in a show she beats him with a shoe. Pennington: "That's assault with a deadly weapon." A dream sequence where Lee comes out of thin air to wow everyone is charming and moodily put together, if rather less creative than you suspect Mann could have dreamt up if he'd given it a few more minutes of thought. But then I guess we never came to know Mann as a director of that particular stripe of florid style; he was always grounded in grim reality, almost never giving into dream logic. The kids playacting adulthood (gossipy, finicky, attention starved adulthood) is a consistent delight. You can see the seeds of everything from *Grease* to *Newsies* to *I'll Do Anything* here, though again, there's no way you could prove anyone had seen it.

Mann still doesn't trust that a camera movement can capture an emotional beat and keeps cutting to close-ups (perhaps not his fault but, as Ford teaches us, there were ways around this sort of thing) when his movement would have sufficed. It's even more impressive that he manages all this crisscrossing movement across cramped sets with teenage actors. He takes in singing performances with easy, patient momentum. Spinning across sets past trees and bodies, jumping to a beautifully weird angle on the roof looking down. Call it his *The Stranger*. The message of domesticity the film promotes is obviously retrograde (and worse because the woman settling down is an over-the-hill actress; no wonder *Sunset Boulevard* was such a phenomenon) but the way Mann captures its particulars makes the medicine go down a little easier.

My Best Gal –1944

By 1944 Anthony Mann was in danger of being typecast as a maker of light comedies and musicals. He proved a steady hand at capturing song and dance by now and it's wild to imagine a time that he becomes the best director of B-movie noir in America (so much so that he'd be called in to rescue *He Walked by Night* in 1948 and shoot b-roll on *Quo Vadis* in '51) and then go back and realize that for a lotta years it was kick lines and backstage teenage drama. It's pretty stupendously disorienting to open up a Mann film with Jane Withers singing and dancing in her shower with the whole neighborhood listening in, almost breaking the fourth wall but laying off just in time. This is the kind of thing Douglas Sirk would do between melodramas. Withers has Judy Garland's over-enunciation and ebullience but lacks her otherworldly charm and insistent innocence. Garland came about those things through trauma and heartbreak so we can't exactly fault Withers for her comparatively heavy footfall, but hey there's a reason you've never heard of her.

She plays a drug store clerk with a brassy voice that keeps everyone nearby compelled. There's enough plot for 19 movies here; a Russian nesting doll of contrivances courtesy of three different screenwriters. Olive Cooper had been writing movies of every stripe since 1935, including Mann's own *Nobody's Darling*, and about a dozen westerns before and after. Earl Fenton was a lightweight till he turned to noir and crime for Richard Fleischer in the 50s, though he didn't last much longer than that. And Richard Brooks (!) became one of the best-known writer/directors of the middle of the century (Jacques Rivette would later group Brooks and Mann with Nicholas Ray ad Robert Aldrich as the best of the post-war directors). I had no clue Brooks was hardening souffle's like this before he broke through with the script for Robert Siodmak's *The Killers* and Jules Dassin's *Brute Force.* Even those were happenstance; he'd done a rewrite on Siodmak's beautifully dunderpated *Cobra Woman,* the movie in which Maria Montez plays twins and not one of them can act. As my friend David Cairns, who is going to come up *a lot* in this volume, once said she can't even *point* properly. It must be seen, along with everything else Siodmak did. Still Brooks rose in no time at all from that to his reputation as the most "literate" of screenwriter, whatever the hell that's supposed to mean, to the undervalued director of *In Cold Blood, Elmer Gantry,* and *Bite The Bullet.* Here you can sense he's just trying to tie the circus tent to the ground a little tighter. Come to think of it a book on Brooks would be worth somebody's time.

Anyway, Withers lives with her grandfather Frank Craven, and starts dating Jimmy Lydon, who wants to write musicals. Yes, eventually they get around to Withers starring in his musicals, but first there's a false betrayal involving a famous producer, a surprise audition, a fatal disease, an army drafting, and trouble at the drugstore. I know I keep using the term "noir" when it was no such thing for many years after its golden age had ended, but there's no denying Mann was crafting films with that exact sensibility. Even here he relies on gorgeous fog lit nights and sporadic neon and shadows cast by venetian blinds. He moves from broad daylight musical numbers before arriving here, of course, but he's quite obviously the director of *Reign of Terror* he just can't prove it yet. The set piece of Kitty performing for a famous producer who's hiding behind the curtain presages *Singing in the Rain;* it's part Shakespeare and part early riff on a wiretapping or eavesdropping that would become de rigueur in genre. There's always an audience for everything Withers does in this one, whether singing or necking with Lydon. It's a very charming version of New York. Everyone's always around the corner with a helping hand and a song. Mann films the hell out of this, dancers falling from the sky, a song on every street. What a kick.

Strangers in the Night – 1944

A view of beautiful islands, then the sound of cannons. Heaven and hell are our settings, which would become *quite* typical for Mann as he veered harder into crime stories and westerns. William Terry is stationed in the South Pacific during the second world war (which was still going when this was made). He's injured and sulking, and not even the letters from his sweetheart Rosemary can console him. He has more reason to be upset than he knows. Rosemary doesn't exist. She's the never-born daughter of batty dowager Helene Thimig. She's been writing to Johnny *as* Rosemary, and with Terry out of commission he might come home to find out for himself just what's going on, with a little help from Virginia Grey, Thimig's new doctor.

Despite the short runtime and Republic Pictures logo upfront this was Mann's most ambitious film. The plotting is fairly relentless, which you'd expect, but it can take you off guard. When the train carrying Terry and Grey during their meet cute *crashes* (!) I almost had a heart attack; critic and filmmaker Gina Telaroli complained of similar symptoms in her piece for MUBI Notebook on the film when it ran during a Scorsese-funded Republic Pictures retrospective in New York. The atmosphere of each environment is perfectly articulated in mere seconds, from the jungle hospital where we meet Terry to the firelit parlor where Thimig's wasting away. The matte painting of the house is marvelous, especially at night, and the shadows are long in this old manor. The cinematographer was Reggie Lanning, but you can sense Mann and John Alton working towards each other, in desperate need of each other's innovations and sensibilities. Make a room huge by externalizing the various derangements chirping away in the minds of its denizens, whether it's Thimig's inconceivable matchmaking or her live-in companion Edith Barrett nervously enabling her.

It's Grey who gets called back up to the big house when Terry collapses after beholding the portrait of Rosemary. Thimig immediately clocks their attraction and has a new reason to loathe Grey beyond her being a lady doctor. The cast is so small (only Anne O'Neal as Grey's nurse Tommy has more than a single scene of dialogue among the support) that it's only a matter of time before the terrible secrets are

14

revealed. Terry's the real problem here, just a dreadfully leaden performer chosen for his baby face not his talent. Grey is marvelous, playing both her budding affection for the marine and her Hawksian maturity in her new job with equal sincerity. Thimig's final act consists mostly of one revelation after another, which does sort of take the wind out of the movie's sails but the impression of the high points lingers, especially considering a magnificent last tableaux: Terry and Grey are conversing in the parlor by firelight, so their shadows are on the sliding doors that Thimig opens, separating the two silhouettes as she means to do to their owners. That's a better last move than her actual plot to kill the young lovers. As usual, a shot says more than a sentence.

The Great Flamarion – 1945

A near two-minute dolly shot takes us from the lobby to the main stage of a Mexico City vaudeville, interrupted by gunshots; this is so wonderful, and Mann knows it, that it gets an encore from a different angle in the final act. The culprit hides in the guts of the theatre as the victim's innocent husband (Steve Barclay) is carted off for the crime. Later that night the killer, Erich Von Stroheim (!), falls out of the rafters and tells his tale of woe to Lester Allen. The shot of him falling is just magnificent and a perfect little B-movie in-joke. Having established that the movie is set in a theatre, we see a heavy figure fall behind a backdrop, a curtain painted to look like a city. Everything is false, just falsehood upon falsehood. Anticipating *Sunset Boulevard* Stroheim plays a once-great sharpshooter who has fallen on hard times. *Also* anticipating *Sunset Boulevard*, this movie was produced by none other than W. Lee Wilder, Billy's idiot brother, whom the mercurial fellow despised after little brother rode his coattails to Hollywood. Not for nothing is this story about infidelity and murder told in flashbacks a la *Double Indemnity*; even when innovating he was stealing. This and the following year's Mann noir *Strange Impersonation* were his first producer credits and the best movies he ever touched. What followed is one of the most hilariously ignominious careers Hollywood ever let slip. "In reality it was the beginning of the end..." muses Stroheim. If only W. Lee had listened.

We go back to his days in Pittsburgh where conniving husband and wife strivers Dan Duryea and Mary Beth Hughes were his assistants, both trying to work him to get one over on the other. The performances oozing from honeyed to acidic depending on what dressing room they're in is as boisterous a spectacle as Stroheim shooting out the lights in his act. Sleazy, sweaty stuff, a stop gap between Joan Crawford's early circus pictures and...Joan Crawford's *late* circus pictures. It's but a matter of time before he misses his mark and kills one of these people. Stroheim's room is full of moving targets that turn into dancing lights on the stars' faces. Stroheim's muscular head (Dave Bautista's the closest we've got to him now but he's of course missing the Austrian's ...*je ne sais quoi...*) sails through the ornate sets like a submarine through a Terry Gilliam decoupage. At one point they actually *shave* the great dome on camera in close-up, daring you to look away from the mountainous thing. Unicyclist's shadows flank serious conversations, mocking them and *always* putting things in the context of performance. Mann isn't *quite* the dynamo of blocking and lighting he was becoming but he's close. There's some *great* business (completely unnecessary but perfect) where Hughes and Stroheim meet on a park bench trying to look inconspicuous but there's a sleeping tramp between them. EvS has to read the newspaper loudly and with maximum elbow to wake him up without appearing to. Just great. Some of that Preston Sturges' nose for human behavior coming through.

Briefly, for no other reason than to celebrate Stroheim's outsized greatness, this quote from a piece I wrote about him for RogerEbert.com:

"...back then, the news of a new movie by Erich von Stroheim was a major event, not least because the public loved reading about the antics of this beleaguered upstart genius. Sixty years before "Heaven's Gate," Stroheim built Monte Carlo in California for "Foolish Wives," bought his actors expensive couture so they'd feel wealthy, insisted he be allowed to eat caviar and drink real champagne on screen, and in the best touch of all, invented a book out of thin air and insisted the movie was adapted from it. Better still, his character, charlatan Count Karamzin sees a diplomat's wife played by Miss DuPont (birth name Patricia Hannon) reading the novel, takes it out of her hands, inspects it, and says "Very good." And he's right to say it. Even the intertitles—"Again Morning … Sapphire sea … Brutality of man … and still the sun"—are pure poetry. There was quite simply no one else like him, and even now, 100 years later, no movie quite like "Foolish Wives."

In 1974, Jonathan Rosenbaum complained that most writing about the legendary Austrian film director and actor Erich von Stroheim got caught up in legends, in the fiction surrounding the Teutonic magpie. No one seemed capable of writing about his movies as works of visual art. Of course, and Rosenbaum concedes as much, this is tough because Stroheim was bigger than life, and he made sure everyone knew it. Young Erich Oswald Stroheim got off a boat to America after fleeing from a dispiriting stint in German military service, changed his name to Erich Oswald Hans Carl Maria von Stroheim und Nordenwall, and introduced himself as a Count, a son of the aristocracy. Nevertheless, he worked menial labor jobs in the heartland before making his way to Hollywood, where he worked his way up from stuntman and assistant to the biggest director and star in the world. It all came crashing down because he tortured everyone while directing, wasted millions of studio money, and refused to make movies less than a full night long. He lied to every reporter he ever talked to, and there were many, to the point that most of his obituaries were running on old half-truths and got crucial details about his life wrong. He spoke with a variety of accents by which everyone who heard it was confused, each believing it betrayed a different region, class, and history.

Stroheim was like the negative image of Charlie Chaplin, a count with no court, and the image of him that survives is as much of the depressive butler hiding behind history with Gloria Swanson in Billy Wilder's *Sunset Boulevard*, or the iron jawed idealist running the POW camp in Jean Renoir's *Grand Illusion*. Just as he used association with D.W. Griffith to his advantage, he was one of the first totems of cinephilia collected by eager young directors desperate to bask in the glow of the image of his twisted genius, a precursor to Wim Wenders' relationship with Nicholas Ray, Peter Bogdanovich's with Orson Welles, and Bogdanovich's with Wes Anderson and Noah Baumbach."

The trouble with calling your movie *The Great Flamarion* is that people have to say the word "Flamarion" every few seconds, which never stops sounding ludicrous; a reminder that a dim fellow indeed put this affair together. "I've had about just as much as I can use outta Flamarion! What is it with you two?" "Me and Flamarion?!" Still, I basically prefer this to *Double Indemnity (and Sunset Boulevard, for that matter)*. It's sleazier, crueler, and quicker. '45 was a hell of a year for noir (*Detour, My Name is Julia Ross, Fallen Angel, Hangover Square, Leave Her to Heaven, Scarlet Street, Mildred Pierce*) and though this isn't up to their level it's a great accent on the house. Mann did his best work in dark corners with desperate, outmatched hopefuls about ten seconds from the final curtain. Stroheim may put on his opera cape, driving gloves, monocle, and top hat, looking like a Teutonic Dracula, but he's as corruptible and destructible as the next man. Very few of us *aren't* in Mann's world.

Two O'Clock Courage – 1945

God bless these 65 minute RKO quickies. Mann went from minor to major looking for paydirt all throughout the 40s, leaving mini-masterpieces in his wake. Likewise the hero of 1945's *Two O'Clock Courage* stumbles into the picture, his back to us, on the corner of Ocean View and Arch looking for his identity. He's been hit hard in the head and can't remember much. He gets into Ann Rutherford's cab (though she almost kills him first; she and the car screeching to a halt at once). "Why do you keep looking through your pockets?" "To find out what's in them." "Serves me right for asking foolish questions!" One of the few times that joke's gotten a laugh out of me. He's Tom Conway, George Sanders' brother, and he was the RKO B-unit's closest thing to a leading man (support in *Cat People* and *I Walked With A Zombie, and owner of one of the saddest stories in Hollywood, born practically into Russian royalty, abandoned by Sanders and his wives because of his drinking, dying in almost complete anonymity in the arms of an old girlfriend, news of his fallen star brief headline fodder for tabloids*). This is a remake of the now forgotten 30s RKO film *Two in the Dark,* whose director Ben Stoloff produces here. Jane Greer makes her debut.

This has a slippery sense of time that's quite ingratiating. We meet Conway in the middle of the night, but it's day-for-night and the scene of him and Rutherford rifling through his belongings has a shimmering sea behind them. It's set *nowhere*, which is perfect for Mann. It's possible that someone says the location sometime but I never caught it and didn't want it. A city with no identity, a man with no identity, and fog-shrouded streets in a nocturnal fugue; this is Mann country, alright. Like the same year's *Detour,* Edgar Ulmer's noir plus ultra, this film makes a virtue of its tiny budget and anonymous setting. This is a more chipper picture, taking cues from Conway's stock character type (the gentleman detective; he played The Falcon in the popular so-named series, also for RKO) and Rutherford's garrulous go-getter cab driver. She's excited to have something interesting to do for the night. Rutherford played second fiddle to another smooth detective, Red Skelton's The Fox, in a few movies so everybody's right at home. Richard Lane and Emory Parnell play two bickering shamuses, one a cop, one a reporter, who shanghai the couple into their investigation after they lie their way into trouble.

"What a yarn I'm gonna write!" Screenwriters Robert E. Kent and Gordon Kahn wrote dozens of B pictures between the two of them, which explains the ratatat of the dialogue and the swiftness of the plot. Kent wrote a handful of Dick Tracy movies and finally at the end of his life, *The Christine Jorgensen Story,* which was also almost Irving Rapper's last movie but for *Sextette* and *Born Again,* two vanity projects for two old queens. This film occasionally gets derailed by comedy business, but never loses its entertaining edge. When the pair go out to a society bar everyone seems to recognize him, but they ought to be more taken with her; she's a four-alarm fire in her dress. It's got kind of a map-print pattern up top and black down satin down to her feet. I may never forget the sight of it. Greer can't help but seem like second best and she's Jane Greer. Conway all but disintegrates to a heap of confetti when stuck improvising with the two of them. You can hardly blame him. Mann's camera sticks largely to wides and long takes to capture the dialogue and the dancing; it's nothing fancy but it more than gets the job done. Then the funniest thing happens: the film laps itself so Conway can finally remember the fateful incident that left him bereft him. His face is superimposed on the crime like Dale Cooper in the final fight scene in *Twin Peaks: The Return.* Still experimenting under all that fuss, Anthony Mann will always surprise you.

Sing Your Way Home – 1945

This one feels like something Godard watched before making *Breathless,* touching upon the broadly sociological vis-à-vis international affairs, freedom of the press, song and dance, and a kinda-sorta hardboiled lead. Jack Haley is a war correspondent for a New York paper looking to get out of Paris now that the war is done, but they can't get him a plane home unless he agrees to chaperone a touring group of young entertainers back to the states. Or they're *supposed* to be young, anyway. The reluctant old fogey has to get hip to the kids hoofing and belting and all their crazy, hep ways if he wants to survive his tenure with them and get home in one piece. Mann would work with Frances Langford, nicknamed The G.I. Nightingale, a year later on *The Bamboo Blonde* and she basically did all this stuff in reality. Mann must have seen that he was being shoehorned into a light comedy corner because in 1947 he'd give up comedy for good.

This was at least partially written by William Bowers, who was *really* good when he was allowed to be, and basically what that means is the film never succumbs to its total weightlessness, though boy it's a close call (the other two writers got up to nothing interesting during their short careers). Haley is no kind of a leading man. Not on screen, anyway, though he might have worked on stage. He looks too much like Emil Jannings to be a romantic lead. He's doing pratfalls by minute 10, Mann having exhausted all he can from the fellow's limited playbook. There's a kind of Marx Brothers-*ish-ness* to the idea of taking a troop of young performers back on a boat to America. They're trying to smuggle one of their passport-less ranks (Marcy McGuire) back without anyone finding out, so they work overtime to provide maximum distraction, throwing pillows around their bedroom and dancing and extemporizing and making use of the shipboard gym equipment (it's kinda like that show Cooper Hoffman does in *Licorice Pizza*). Haley and Anne Jeffreys have to romance each other while basically never making eye contact; they're deeply weird performers, all rubber band mannerisms and too-practiced sarcasm. These aren't people you'd mistake for human, which is why we needed Godard to cast the unpracticed likes of Anna Karina and Sami Frey to embody those types and make them real.

Mann is hamstrung by the tiny sets and the lack of real intrigue in the plot so he once more relies on mediums and wides and keeps the camera running as long as he can. There are a couple of cursive tracking shots that keep you awake if the sound of stomping and singing and pouting teens doesn't do the trick. There's a bewitching little number where Jeffreys sings the kids to sleep while closing curtains between their beds, and a pretty good shower-set tap dancing number. Haley's constant humiliation can be funny but not as a rule (one of them hinges on a passenger ship having a bookstore…?). The most Bowers line in the piece finds Haley being his pompous, humorless self when Jeffreys scolds him about giving the troop some of his upcoming airtime during a radio broadcast. "These kids grew up in show business, why giving them a chance to perform is like giving a drink to a starving drunk." A little dramatic, no? Wasn't there just a war happening? Has no one learned anything? Don't answer that.

Strange Impersonation – 1946

W. Lee Wilder's last failed attempt to cross over into A pictures before deciding that B's (well... I don't know, D's or F's is maybe more accurate) were easier is a peculiar film indeed. The plot is so fucking crazy you can't sum it up in less than a paragraph but broadly it's about Hillary Brooke and Ruth Ford trying to ruin Brenda Marshall's life, one with blackmail, the other with disfiguration. Brooke wants William Gargan, Marshall's boyfriend, for herself. "Why?" is truly anyone's guess, the man is barely animate; truly and deeply uninteresting. When he limply throws himself at Marshall for the first time she's aghast. "Stephen..." she says, indicating all the beakers and test tubes. "...remember science!" What on earth this is meant to indicate, I could not say. Is the implication that you're not allowed to neck in front of an experiment for fear it may be halfway to sentience? Doesn't science make room for sexual reproduction? Isn't that the whole p… better to let it go.

The rest of the movie has the same "we need a scene here..."improvisational quality. Marshall's leaving work one day (she's a brain doctor) and almost hits Ford with her car. George Chandler sees this and makes it his personal crusade to get Ford to extort Marshall for all she's worth, having waited his entire life for his destiny to make itself clear. Really strange idea and Chandler's insistent performance makes it nightmarish. Scenarist Mindret Lord (!) is a figure of complete mystery, with a dozen best guesses making up the bulk of his biography. Was he involved in the Leopold and Loeb case? Was he Rabindranath Tagore's nephew? Was his name an anagram for Dorm Tendril? Evidently no one knows for sure, but his penchant for byzantine pulp stories is evident.

Mann directs this bizarre little melodrama pretty impressively. It opens with a magnificent dolly shot across a lecture hall, its blocking always hints at the dynamics between characters, and makes great use of graphic lines in every environment. He constantly frames Marshall in mirrors during the first act to presage her fate in the third. Brooke disfigures Marshall in a chemical explosion to make her so ugly that Gargan will leave her (normal stuff). Marshall and Brooke do risky experiments on themselves in their own home, which gives Brooke the window she needs to light her boss on fire. She all but insists Gargan leave her now that she's been deep fried, but he's stubborn in his affection (and boy does the screen positively sizzle when he is. "Just which one of these two has been a human chemical fire, anyway?!" the critics did not ask at the time of its negligible release). Somehow no one thinks to ask why Brooke needed to do that specific hazardous mixture while Marshall was sleeping, but Brooke immediately conspires to break the two up, and everyone at the hospital enables this for some reason. What is even less clear is how Brooke plans to make this plan work after Marshall gets out of the hospital. Mary Treen plays a nurse and seems to have been convinced this was going to be her big break as she clomps all over her scenes like one of the singing teens in Mann's musicals. Everyone in this movie is too nosy for their own good.

When Ford re-enters the story she's got a whole new personality. She decides to rob

Marshall at gunpoint (which doesn't strike me as sound legal action, but what do I know?) and ends up a stain on the sidewalk beneath Marshall's apartment window for her trouble. Of course, she's wearing a ton of Marshall's jewelry so everyone thinks Marshall committed suicide, which allows her to start her life over *as* Ford's lush blackmailer. Mann films the plastic surgery that grants her a new identity in suitably expressionist fashion. The movie was made for zero dollars but he does good work on the cardboard sets. The surgery and recovery take a year for some reason and when she emerges she's a brunette but otherwise identical. When she comes back for revenge Gargan and Brooke are married. It turns out she doesn't have *much* of a plan. She gets her old job back and then months later confronts the usurper and threatens to kill her if she doesn't leave Gargan. Status quo reattained. Almost like the whole thing never happened. Of course, there are still ten minutes left. Plenty of time for a cruel twist if you haven't injured yourself trying to wake up.

The Bamboo Blonde –1946

If you're a fan of the phrase "Bamboo Blonde," and at this point I'd like to think you are, this is 2025 after all, boy oh boy, do I have a movie for you. Walter Reed shows up to interview Ralph Edwards about his business empire. He has a successful line of cosmetics, clothes, drinks, you name it. Just how did he do it? It's a long story, with many twists and turns, and it starts with well-to-do Russell Wade getting stood up by Jane Greer. Wade's parents are from Bucks County, PA (like me!) so you just know they're wealthy (he writes from a basement apartment). Wade's junior officer on his flight crew (Glen Vernon) and the rest of the boys have some kind of scheme cooked up to embarrass their commander. They send him to a nightclub where no one's happy to see him, which is a mystery to him, but it's because the club is on the Military Police blacklist. Servicemen keep drinking there and listening to Frances Langford sing in her black cocktail dress, and it's bad for morale. Wade waits in the alley to tell his hard luck story to Langford, who takes pity on him and takes him for a drink where they end up dancing, which makes the staff at this new bar nervous, and she sees him off to the war with a kiss and no first names exchanged. You starting to get the very insistent and yet weightless vibe of this one yet? If you're not in the right mood this'll give you a headache

Screenwriters Lawrence Kimble and Olive Cooper kept busy for their years behind the typewriter, though never became A picture specialists. Cooper was on the verge of becoming Anthony Mann's favourite screenwriter when she retired in 1950. She was George Stevens' aunt and their whole family were actors and directors. This movie has "quick paycheck" written all over it. Evidently it was based on a story by the otherwise unknown-to-me Wayne Whittaker, and it's a kind of proto-*La Ronde* about the way chance encounters can influence crazy events down the line, but it's not rangy enough for that comparison to quite work. I was waiting for the focus to shift and the cast to expand, but that didn't really happen. Eventually we get to the plot, such as it is. Wade has Vernon draw Langford on the side of their bomber, she becomes their good luck charm as the plane kills hundreds of people, they make it into Time Life magazine and Langford sees it and her nightclub incorporates it into her act, which boosts drink and ticket sales like crazy.

The real trouble here is that Mann didn't find any work to do. It's perfectly well staged of course, and moves at quite the clip, but it's just not the kind of movie you can do much with without turning it avant-garde, which he should have done. RKO would have let him, I can't help but think. This was the house of Val Lewton after all, a man who never met a producer who liked losing money on art. But after a while you have to just let the tide take you. There's a new development or dramatic irony or mistaken identity or some other contrivance every other scene. He does good work with a late music number involving a standee of Wade and a bedroom set but mostly he's just keeping up with the blocking. Tough to get anything done when you're busy being a doorman for the script. Right this way, madame, just over here. The dialogue flies so fast in this, you barely have time to register the absurd mid-Atlantic mispronunciations (among other things,

Langford doesn't like "Ulti*MAH*tums")
There's 25 minutes left of the movie when
the bulk of the loose ends have been tied
up. Both Langford and Wade get the jitters
as their inevitable reunion looms, having
both pretended to be engaged during the
war, not least because Greer *also* reads
about their fake engagement and decides
to reclaim Wade now that he's famous. She
chases Langford away by saying she'll tell
everyone Wade's secretly rich. Not really
sure that's the bombshell she imagines it is,
but I guess neither is she if Wade won't
throw Langford over for her. Even at only
67 minutes you want it to be a little more
fleet.

Desperate – 1947

The first shot finds a little kid ambushing
our hero, Steve Brodie, on the street with a
toy gun, a warning about what's coming to
him. His wife, Audrey Long, is pregnant and
violence is about to define their life. Brodie
gets offered some quick cash and winds up
an accessory to robbery and murder in no

time at all. Gangster Raymond Burr decides he's going to make sure Brodie pays for the screw-up that results when he tries to do the right thing and winds up getting a bunch of cops and crooks killed. If he wants Long to live through the night he has to go down to police headquarters and take the rap, though of course he flees with her instead on the train. The chase is on. Can they stay alive long enough to have their baby?

This was Mann's first real noir and he liked what the genre allowed him to do. Finally, the trouble with which his heroes were dealing was rooted in a kind of reality. A simple thing, but just the moment-to-moment stress of "I have to get off this train before someone recognizes me" is so much more concrete than "I'm flirting with a singer while chaperoning a gang of teenagers across the ocean" or "my rival has scarred me with acid to steal my boyfriend." He did fine work with these movie plots but noir's external simplicity and internal torment allowed him to think psychologically, which his byzantine comedies and proto-noir hadn't. The camera can tell a story and burrow deep into the mind. He uses swinging overhead light and low angles during conflagrations and interrogations and then close-ups whenever he has an important interaction between the young lovers (who have pretty shocking chemistry; you believe they want to jump each other as much as you like their cute interactions). Some of this style must be cost consciousness but it works. They're trapped with each other and the world is out there, eager to make them the criminals they so...uhh, *fervently* want not to be.

George E. Diskant is the photographer (John Alton still two films away) and his key lighting and shadows aren't precise enough but you get a decent enough idea of a world in crisis, of the Edenic paradise of a couple of lower middle class strivers interrupted by criminal greed. Mann's quick-witted and cynically urban sensibility means that the trip to the countryside (complete with beautiful barn-set wedding, looking like the centerpiece of *The Village* some 60 years later) they take to escape will be short lived and unreliable. Jason Robards Sr, whose son of course grew into his laconic manner, plays the cop who pursues Brodie. "For every ten guys who go to the chair, six go crying "innocent."" Crying innocent is something Mann's heroes would do, inside or out, from here on out. Few of them would mean it. The finale has a pretty stark last clash between Brodie and Burr that becomes Mann's raison d'etre. The man with the gun to his head, and the man who's listening to the sound of a clock...counting down his last seconds. "Who was it said "time flies"?" Asks Burr, the clock so loud it overtakes even the music on the score. Terrifically grim. Mann's second act begins.

Railroaded! – 1947

Moving from RKO to PRC would have been a considerable step down for everybody except Anthony Mann, who by now was so good he could work on any budget (and indeed he had). Producers Releasing Corporation was one of the unlucky 13, the dingy little studios who made movies for pennies collectively dubbed Poverty Row. Republic Pictures produced its fair share of masterpieces by accidentally throwing money at talented hands (John Ford, Orson Welles, Nicholas Ray) who couldn't find money elsewhere while PRC and Monogram were probably the most infamous. This opens with a cheap paper cityscape but then the camera's zoom turns into a smooth dolly down a street introducing our anti-heroes. There's Jane Randolph, the sassy, exhausted manager of a beauty parlor, and the two men here to "rob" the place while she lets them. It's her score, ya see, and now the only thing that could screw it up is...well everything. Mann shoots the chaos as a series of Eisensteinian close-ups of quick action, hiding the budget. A gun barrel shoving its way into frame and focus, a woman screaming and grabbing a curtain as she falls into terrified unconsciousness, a window being shot up, one of the trigger men dying as his partner runs in behind him to take care of the cop who stumbled onto the robbery. As in *Desperate,* the hero is a guy who wasn't involved in the crime. They're gonna pin it once more on a truck driver, this time played by Ed Kelly. John Ireland explains this to Keefe Brasselle in intense, deep shadow in the front seat of the car. They look like they're about to start passionately necking.

When Kelly's life is about to become a noir plot he and his sister (Sheila Ryan) are discussing a crime film they just saw and discussing what right the police have to do harm against people. This kind of slight meta-textual observance is part and parcel with Mann going forward, who would admit up front with every one of his films that you're just watching one possible interpretation of these events: the best one. In *Reign of Terror* and *The Tall Target* you're asked to believe cramped studios are really the settings of revolution. *Railroaded!* is based on the same criminal case as Henry Hathaway's *Call Northside 777* from the next year; Joseph Majczek and Theodore Marcinkiewicz were arrested in 1933 for murdering a cop they didn't murder and spent ten years in stir for it, before it was revealed that the evidence wasn't legit and corruption had abetted the conviction. Imagine that. Knowing this it's only a matter of time before Kelly gets picked up looking guilty.

Mann's movies have the feeling of something both personal and impersonal, like a keepsake kept in his wallet. Everyone's got one, but only his are like this. The table with the light in it on which Kelly's fingerprints are extracted feels like the kind of gadget only he would have created, for instance. The domestic scenes have a thin and fast character, Mann saving the fireworks for the more intense scenes. John C. Higgins's dialogue can be *real* good. Kelly doesn't seem like much to behold but he handles some of this very well. When asked to take things seriously by a lawyer he says killing a man isn't a joke, not even a cop. "Don't like cops, eh?" "No, I'm gettin' real attached to you guys." Ryan goes to confront Randolph and a *savage* cat fight breaks out, which Ireland watches, bemused, from the dark room next door, knowing he can't reveal himself or he'll have to kill Ryan to keep her from knowing he was involved. Ireland tries to menace her personally later on a crowded dance floor, a terrific sequence, but she's also being pursued by the lead detective on the case, Hugh Beaumont. Now her proving her brother's innocence has an erotic dimension broiling just beneath it. "You're a

dame, arencha?" "I don't like that word."
When the only semi-reliable witness is
killed (about seventeen different ways, to
hear the coroner tell it) the stakes ratchet
up a notch without much having changed.
Skillfully handled interpersonal drama and
simmering resentment between familiars. It
can only end with bullets.

T-Men – 1947

There was a short-lived vogue for true
crime stories in the US cinema that then
found its way to the small screen. And I
don't simply mean "ripped from the
headlines" but rather with the cooperation
of and on-screen appearance of officials
who really worked in law enforcement. This
opens with the most unpromising sight of
the lumpen mug of Elmer Lincoln Irey of the
United States Treasury Department. He's
got a piece of paper in front of him with
some bullet points about the goings on
within his office, six teams of "shock troops"
on standby (you wouldn't think someone
could make that sound boring but Elmer

manages). Just as you begin to reach for a pillow and blanket, the film itself actually starts and John Alton fires up the monochrome neon and shadows and it's the most beautiful sight in the world. A heist in abstraction, faces peering from the darkness, a gas works like the one in Ozu's *Hen in the Wind,* furtive glances, gun shots from inside the massive bulk of unseen assassins, men running, cars departing... Anthony Mann reborn. Even the exposition looks stunning.

Art Smith and Herbert Hayes need someone to go undercover to infiltrate the Detroit mob and Alfred Ryder and Dennis O'Keefe are the lucky duo who get the job. Mann relies on montage as much as scene craft, but imbues each image with life, from odd geometric angles intersecting (car door and an office building) to the brimming, bright light and busy sights of a hallway in a public records office visible just because a door is left open behind our heroes. Every scene takes place in front of its own junior scene, like a diorama. Casting character actors and comedians to play cops and crooks pays rich dividends because it encourages you to put the faces into the frame and not view them as stars but as more moving parts. Lots of incredible faces in this one. Jack Overman, Charles McGraw, Wallace Ford, William Malten, John Wengraf, Tito Vuolo... more slopes and peaks and crags than Mount Baldy.

The camera angles are repurposed, of course, from German Expressionism, adding to every interaction a Caligarian sense that everything is *wrong*, that these are bad, warped men. Wellesian feverishness sets in during scenes in bathhouses and dark alleys. Tempting to wonder what Mann would have made if he'd had Welles' ambition and particular tastes. The documentary aspect, the unobtrusive camera in some settings, makes the violence that breaks out seem like the real thing, kinda like Stanley Kubrick's coverage of the military engagement in *Dr. Strangelove*. Alton and Mann lose track of the throng of guys, very few of whom we know anyway. The interrogations and shakedowns look like details from a lost Goya, and the desire to shoot things in a way no one else would have thought sounds like novelty, but it matches the pace and tone like a glove.

Light comes to seem like an invasive species, a nuisance; too much, all the time. The ceiling is always visible because everyone must always feel trapped and it's proof that there's no heaven up there. Just concrete and drywall.

The underworld is meant to be alien to the viewer - taking the prologue at face value that audience members would be seeing it for the first time, the excitement of discovery is twofold: a version of life never before glimpsed by polite society (tough not to picture John Dillinger watching *Manhattan Melodrama* in *Public Enemies*) *and* a cinema to match. Mann likely wasn't thinking of the long view so much as he was thinking of how best to approach this script, but he gave permission to the later likes of Michael Mann and David Fincher to turn their genre pieces into expressionist boleros. And the amazing thing is this was just the beginning of a six-film streak that would quietly reshape the American cinema.

Raw Deal – 1948

Raymond Burr's first big part was in André de Toth's *Pitfall* and it's one of the best bits of acting of the 1940s. He has a monologue he delivers, his massive bulk's every corner stuffed oddly into a suit so large it hinges on a novelty like David Byrne in *Stop Making Sense*, as he's packing Lizabeth Scott's things, preparing them both for a new life she doesn't want. He knows she doesn't want it, but she'll accept it, because that's what happens. We settle. We settle for men like Burr. A blistering bit of self-loathing. I bring this up because his turn in *Raw Deal* was the penultimate performance of his unknown-phase, and he's good but we see why he needed *Pitfall*. We see him first in a robe with a long cigarette looking very much like a Welles villain. He's good value, a kind of special effect, another minor American Emil Jannings, but he shares the 'heavy' lifting with John Ireland and Curt Conway even if he's the big bad in his silk Sulka, burning women with flaming Courvoisier before Lee Marvin ever boiled coffee for Gloria Grahame.

Raw Deal is a Fritz Lang-esque tripod opera, with crazed angles and graphic upset, shadows bisecting faces and rooms like a scimitar. Pure noir in other words. Two women (Clare Trevor and Marsha Hunt) visit Dennis O'Keefe in prison. One of them is troubled to see him, the other elated. One's obsessed with him but can't decide how she really feels. The other is breaking him out to be with him. The way O'Keefe exhales when the two women trade places in the visitation room is its own short story. Burr has told O'Keefe he'll spring him from the joint because he took the fall for the big guy. Of course, it's not to be. Burr has planned one trap after another for him to spring during the escape, hoping he'll die before Burr ever has to pay him for his services. Trevor is along for the ride, though he breaks into social worker Hunt's apartment first thing to see about this sexual tension they've been harboring.

Every set of blinds, arrangement of telephone wires, or piece of fencing looks like prison bars. Hunt tries to appeal to his softer nature but he's buried it pretty good after years as a juvenile delinquent and then a full-fledged hood. With Trevor and

Hunt on either shoulder, O'Keefe has to decide who he really is. Though this period of Mann's filmography is filled to a point of pure purpose, there's much character down those jagged compositions. O'Keefe has Trevor help Hunt get dressed "Muuust I?" she whines. Trevor narrates, which is a *weird* choice and a good one. She's the only one whose psychology isn't the point of the film. She's besotted and willing to do anything to prove it. Not terribly complicated, whereas O'Keefe is our tortured hero burying his nicer self with every mile as Hunt is trying to keep his head above the dirt. Photography of a forest is pure poetry, with John Alton weighing silhouettes and smoke dancing against the night sky. Alton is plainly thrilled to be using real sunlight and smoke and he expands the film beyond its 1.33:1 frame. 1948 was probably the banner year for American noir, and this has much in common with Negulesco's *Road House,* another A+ B picture, with its camping trips and battles of the sexes.

Maybe the best wrinkle in the plot is that the police are chasing *two* criminals while O'Keefe is on the lam. Whit Bissell killed a woman who didn't want him, and he winds up at O'Keefe's hideout. Just as Hunt and Trevor are doubles, O'Keefe finds his own double in Bissell's ranting, gibbering maniac who would rather die than keep swallowing his guilt. "That could be you," Hunt says unnecessarily. Noir is all about the dark double, the evil potential, the twin we hide inside each of us ready to jump out and act on all our buried impulses (literally in the case of Robert Siodmak's *The Dark Mirror*). Like *Moonrise, Frank* Borzage's near-noir from the same year, we see the difficult business of keeping that devil inside you. When Ireland is sent to kill O'Keefe, the latter is framed with hands up in the shadow of a stuffed bear striking the same pose. A couple of seconds, a hitch in your plan, that look on Hunt's face of bitter ecstasy when she kills for O'Keefe, a step to the left, a hair out of place, and you could be an ornament instead of an animal, the hero or a bit player, angel or devil.

He Walked By Night - 1948

"The names have been changed to protect the innocent..." Yes, this was the movie that inspired *Dragnet*. *Co-star* Jack Webb was so inspired by conversations with technical advisor Marty Wynn that he started jotting down ideas for a police procedural unlike any other, where the real nitty gritty of solving crimes takes precedence over spectacle and personal drama. The show is still fun to watch in small doses, but the film could have used a little more of both. I blame original director Alfred L. Werker (Mann was brought on midway through production, though when and where is hard to determine) for the film's straight forward presentation of the facts when Mann's harrowing abstraction would have paid richer dividends. The only Werker film I've seen is a patch job (he directed a third of T*he Reluctant Dragon,* and like a lot of this it's dryly procedural. Robert Benchley taking a tour of the Disney studios before meeting Uncle Walt himself - hardly the stuff of abrogated reality that had lately come to seep into Mann's work and would rip the roof right off *Reign of Terror,* his next movie).

Starts magnificently, I must say, with Richard Basehart shooting a cop on a dark street, precipitating one motherfucker of a car crash. But the dry direction of the investigation just doesn't sing like Mann's earlier *T-Men,* this movie's obvious inspiration. It's tempting to say all the scenes with good compositions and eerie, productive use of silence are Mann's, but in fairness I have no sense of Werker's style, if indeed he had any. The only film of his I can claim to have seen is *The Reluctant Dragon, of* which he only shot a couple of dry minutes, and that's a movie with no dramatic plot at all. The important factor here is John Alton, Mann's new favourite cinematographer, the man who perfected American noir lighting. Even if the film was all Werker's doing it was still going to look great, and it does, despite a couple of bafflingly dull blocking and framing choices, like the one of Basehart patching a gunshot wound, shot with his heaving chest and face the only things visible above a bowl of steaming water. Odd stuff...

The cast is magnificent, all in-fielders who never took the spotlight. Webb and Basehart, of course, but also Scott Brady,

Roy Roberts, Whit Bissell, James Cardwell, Byron Foulger, John Dehner, Frank Cady and Kenneth Tobey; men with ten pounds of face each. Werker and Mann do occasionally frame for maximum sweaty paranoia. A scene of witnesses identifying a sketch of Basehart recalls the newspapermen debriefing after the newsreel in *Citizen Kane.* If the film were freer with space and tone, it could have touched Welles' coattails, like the best of Mann (the two seemed in conversation and sometimes Mann even bested him, which is no mean feat). The scenes in the LA sewers are awe-inspiring (though could do without all the damned narration) and they pre-empt *Them!,* Joseph Losey's *M remake,* and *The Third Man* the following year. It's a work smack dab in the middle of generic invention, not quite coining enough to become notable, but reaching its tendrils in every direction and feeling some interesting texture. It'd be a good film to screenshot to highlight what it gets right, but it only gets a head of steam going once every fifteen minutes, usually when Basehart kills. His interrogation of Bissell in his home is pretty heart-stopping, and the film's relative lack of music becomes a virtue.

This, like some of *Dragnet*, was based on a real case, the insane story of Erwin Walker, or "Machine Gun" Walker. He'd been at Leyte during the second world war and had seen a lot of his friends cut to pieces by enemy bayonets, which seems to have snapped a spring in his head. He started stealing guns when he got back to the states, then stealing any and everything he could to pay for his biggest scheme yet. He had a cockeyed idea he was going to build a kind of laser out of movie sound equipment and radar pieces and hold the government hostage until they raised solder's wages, kind of like Ed Harris in *The Rock*. He tried to sell a lot of microphones and stuff to a sound engineer, who knew it couldn't have been gotten legally and called the police. It took a year for police to put an end to his reign of terror. He plead insanity, but the judge wasn't having any of that, so Walker and his father both tried to commit suicide; Walker's attempt wasn't successful, his father's was. The suicide got his death sentence postponed, and by the time they got around to re-scheduling they commuted it to life in prison, but that was *also* commuted, and he was released in 1974, at which point he changed his name and became a chemist. He died in 2008. I think he warranted a weirder movie, but the one he got was pretty good.

Reign of Terror or The Black Book – 1949

There is only one *Reign of Terror. Many movies share its DNA, many movies seem to escape from its smoking ruins, but the experience of watching it remains fully singular.* Anthony Mann used to demur in interviews when accused of being an artist, but this stretch from 1948 to 1952 proves otherwise. The things he achieved while remaining in the confines of what a mini-major would want to sell to audiences is nothing short of remarkable and smack dab in the middle is one of the best low budget movies ever made, a Wellesian feat of ingenuity, psychological abstraction, and shocking formal brio. *Reign of Terror* is as good a movie as *Citizen Kane*, though it's almost ludicrous to compare them as their aims were so different. *Kane* was an attempt to bring Welles's own brand of theatrical storytelling from radio to the big screen, manipulating an audience's understanding of how information is consumed to toss them about a sea of tragic character flaws, used a hundred years of theatrical tradition to show that the kings and queens about whom every day dramas used to be written were now crooked media moguls - which is a longwinded way of saying Welles saw that America's political life would be tied to the image more than the idea (whereas sadly the cinema would reverse this in the 21st century). Mann's aims were simpler: make an epic for less than a million dollars. The script was originally for a very conventional film, a series of speeches as the Reign of Terror took hold in France. Mann realized it was conventional (and dull), so he and screenwriter Philip Yordan rewrote it, and William Cameron Menzies came aboard to design the shots, which cameraman John Alton would then turn to arch visual poetry, the finest in America since Josef Von Sternberg met Marlene Dietrich, with all the sensual close-ups, palace intrigue, and maimed bodies that implies.

A long, long word about William Cameron Menzies from my 7-part biographical series on him at The Maze: "The section of Park Street where William Charles Menzies in 1896 is home now to a few charming old brick buildings, bare lots, and stern apartment buildings. Much of New Haven is in thrall to the demands of nearby Yale University, and indeed it feels like a disused alley for sleepless students, a neighborhood re-fitted for progress that never arrived. Menzies may not have recognized this street some one hundred and thirty years after his birth, as he would not recognize the cinema he pioneered, but he would have felt it in his bones. For Menzies was a man who saw the future, and it looked like a nightmare. In his essential biography *William Cameron Menzies: The Shape of Films to Come* author James Curtis writes that Menzies spent a formative year in his ancestral Scottish village, growing used to the idea that some untouchable natural world, of fairies and daemons, was just out of reach on the fog strewn heath. The bleakness of

New Haven, the haunted Scottish hinterland – they'd recur throughout his work as a director, whether in the Lovecraftian nightmare story *The Maze* or in the awe-inspiring early special effects film *Things to Come*; Menzies never forget what it felt like to be a child seeing the work of history. His most famous work as a director, *Invaders from Mars*, is one of the truest films about childhood Hollywood ever produced. A young boy's horrified perspective of the world of adults, perverted and warped, is what makes *Invaders* the uncanny film it is.

Menzies started drawing at a young age, inspired by the folklore of that Scottish hamlet and its vast medieval death toll. He drew more than he studied. His father encouraged him, with a warning. "…as soon as you earn your first penny by art I'll stop your allowance." So best be good. He decamped to New York's Art Students League and a cramped, frequently freezing little apartment. The long faced young Bill was still nobody's idea of a model student, doing his homework late at night after wasting a day drinking 22 cent bourbon. Menzies started paying attention in class when the famous social realist painter Robert Henri showed up. The Ohio-born Henri was only ten years from his death when he started his conversations with Bill. He had been a rebellious figure in the American art world, a hellraising independent, part-Van Gogh, part-Toulouse-Lautrec. It's easy to spy works like Henri's 1909 *Salome* in the production design work Menzies would later perform on frothy entertainments like *The Spider* and *The Thief of Bagdad*. Henri's other students included George Bellows and Edward Hopper, who are each better respected in the field of the visual arts than Menzies, which shows some of the bias against filmic design work in art history.

Menzies studied under Charles Chapman and Harvey Dunn at their private school in Leonia, NJ whenever the league wasn't in session where he rubbed elbows with other students like N.C. Wyeth, whose own work would take on the mythic in a way not at all dissimilar to Menzies. Wyeth paintings of giants, Buffalo Bill, Francis Drake, Lancelot, King Arthur, Billy Bones and Robinson Crusoe had exactly the boisterous, boyish feel of the best of Menzies' design work.

Just as his father cut him off as he was making money drawing for hardware catalogues and the like, he met a Polish artist named Anton Grot at Hendrick's restaurant on 56th in Manhattan. Grot was a painter, too, except he had a job working in the movies. Grot wanted to hire Menzies' roommate, but he had enlisted and wasn't available, so Menzies reported to Solax Studios in Fort Lee, NJ, assisting Grot on the preparation for the sets of a George Fitzmaurice film called *The Naulahka* (which wouldn't be released until 1918 thanks to editing delays). Grot had presented "Fitz" with the idea of forced perspective, which was all well and good but that meant painting 60-foot-high sets. That's where Bill came in. While Grot was painting sets, Bill was dummying up palm trees shadows in a miserable corner of New Jersey.

Soon Menzies was directing sequences in his and his friend's apartments to get the inserts and backgrounds done on time, learning how to make movies with enormous speed and efficiency. Two more Fitzmaurice films followed, *The Mark of Cain* (1917) and *Innocent* (1918), and then a quick change of pace: marriage to a woman named Mignon Toby and the Merchant Marines, which saw him return to Scotland as part of his assignment at sea. This only lasted a few months, though the marriage, however strained it became, lasted until his death. He started freelancing as an illustrator for advertising firms once again. He did this for as long as he could stand it before fate threw him a bone; he ran into his George Fitzmaurice once more, who got him a gig working at producer Jesse Lasky's Famous Players studio, just two blocks from his and his wife's apartment on 58th street.

Menzies impressed the star of a film that would eventually be called The Test of Honor: John Barrymore in his first dramatic leading role. Barrymore's favor got Menzies a raise and a promotion. Soon he'd be designing sets for two movies a month for Famous Players. A studio like Famous Players couldn't afford (or house) the grand sets of something like a D.W. Griffith production and so a man like Menzies was worth his weight in gold. He could design sets that could trick the eye better than anyone. As Art Nouveau gave way to design trends like futurism and Art Deco in the teens and twenties, so did motion pictures begin to rely on the same visual intricacy in their staging. Movies could no longer just be people in rooms; they had to...well, *move*. Menzies was sent to England to head of design at Famous Players' new (and still under construction) studio there, but no work materialized so he returned to New York. He took an offer from Raoul Walsh to start designing for him at twice his usual rate just as he was about to return to advertising.

Their first film together, *The Deep Purple*, is missing, but what is known is that it wasn't much of a success. As it had been Walsh's idea, he decided to give star his wife and star Miriam Cooper control over their next project, and she chose to make a melodrama called *The Oath*, which flopped even worse than *The Deep Purple*. Curtis suggests that working with Lubitsch on Mary Pickford's first serious drama *Rosita* had awoken in him the idea that the European way of set design (think of the set design in a film like Robert Weine's foundational expressionist work *The Cabinet of Dr. Caligari* (which I recognize

I've already mentioned, but hey, nobody's perfect!), in which the sets dictate nearly everything, from mood to action to character and plot reveals) was the way forward, the only way he'd ever feel truly satisfied with his creations. Not as mere backdrops, but as characters, as story. Fairbanks was cooking up just such a chance for him as he was plotting this new phase of his career, starting with *The Thief of Bagdad*, their biggest hit to date, and made immortal by Menzies' sets. He would start directing after a few more high-profile and big budget movies, first having gone to Europe to help make movies for the war effort, including a remake of *Bagdad,* which he designed with an even more rich palette.

Menzies' reputation grew and grew to the point where some critics would sight him in their reviews and producers stopped caring what director was assigned to his projects because his work was so thorough he would already have done the visual heavy lifting. Directorial efforts like *Things to Come* and *Chandu The Magician* had showed him capable of working his magic without a more experienced director on hand, but he was nevertheless not trusted with dialogue, which was usually handled by Sam Wood. The obvious joke about his last name was sometimes too good to refuse, though I stand by their film of Thornton Wilder's *Our Town*.

Menzies fortunes were on the wan in the mid-40s, so it's no surprise he was eyeing an escape route. He worked on a movie called *Deadline at Dawn* with a theatre director named Harold Clurman making his picture debut, and his movies with and without Sam Wood were making less and less money. Producer David O. Selznick still valued him (he'd had him do reshoots on Hitchcock's *Spellbound* (1945) and brought him into do about five days' work on the troubled *Duel in the Sun* [1946] shoot) but that value went down every time one of his movies went into the red. Frank Capra had come back from active duty to direct *It's a Wonderful Life* (also '46) and once more hired Menzies to help him design some things. Capra wanted Menzies to make the heaven sequences less maudlin in their design but wound up keeping the designer on set with him almost as a crutch while he got his legs back under him after so long a hiatus.

Menzies was also working with Lewis Milestone on *Arch of Triumph* near simultaneously. He was overtaxed and receiving very little in the way of credit. He and Wood made *Ivy* together in 1947 with Joan Fontaine when both productions ceased, and though the film is an astonishment visually, apparently Wood was coming to his end as a useful collaborator for Menzies, who had relied on him to work with the actors while he designed the look of the film. Fontaine remembered Wood as being practically mute. Their relationship grew silently strained with Menzies drinking heavily after filming every night and Wood unable to help or rein him in. They hadn't been estranged for more than a year and a half when Wood died of a sudden heart attack. He was 66, only six years older than Menzies would be when he joined him in death a few years later. Both films would eventually finish but fall into obscurity almost immediately.

It was under these troubled circumstances that Menzies was casting about wildly for a project in the late 40s. Treatments were being snubbed, his release credits were weighing him down, a proposed TV program of short films he was producing was turned down because of proposed costs, and anyway no one seemed sure what was going to be a hit or not anymore. It was only ingenuity that produced his next film. His most recent script had been rejected and, while he still had producer Walter Wanger's ear, he suggested they shoot something fast on the still standing sets of his most recent failure, *Joan of Arc* with Ingrid Bergman. They grabbed a script for a project called *The Bastille*, French in setting so the sets wouldn't need to be altered, gutted it for parts and built a potboiler right into the middle of it like an ectopic pregnancy. The resulting film, *Reign of Terror,* cost about as much as a single day's shooting on *Ivy*, but was designed by Menzies, directed by Anthony Mann, and photographed by John Alton, so it turned out to be one of the best movies of the decade, still the kind of perfect B movie against which all others must be judged."

Menzies was dead not even ten years later of cancer after a lifetime of boozing and overwork with one last overdue accolade for the wrong film. He had helped produce

Around the World in 80 Days (1956), which won best picture at that year's academy awards. *Wicked* winning this year would be as fitting a tribute, if not to Menzies' genius than to the Academy's taste, as I can imagine.

Black Book was a production of Eagle-Lion Films, a subsidiary of Pathé Industries, a creation meant to bolster the legendary and polarizing French film studio after the war. Pathé, founded in 1896, opened its doors to British producer J. Arthur Rank after the conclusion of the Second World War. Joseph Arthur Rank, 1st Baron Rank was born into Victorian elegance in 1888 to a flour mill magnate. J. Arthur as he became known professionally was put in charge of his father's flour mill, though Joseph Sr. had little confidence in his boy. The company would become Hovis, and particularly weird and obsessive cinema students will know it as the company for which Ridley Scott directed a landmark spot, his second most famous advertisement, in the mid-70s. Rank, a devoted Methodist, read in the Methodist papers (when such things evidently got better circulation) that Britain needed more homegrown film product. Dutifully, he approached some other likeminded millionaires and started producing and distributing British films. He bought the Odeon Cinemas chain and the Amalgamated Studios in Borehamwood, then decided to conquer America.

Sensing a kindred spirit in super producer David O. Selznick, Rank bought the rights to his films in re-release, bought up the American poverty row studio Producers Releasing Corporation, and joined Pathé in time for the studio to begin marketing to Americans. This American arm of the European ventures would become Eagle-Lion and their first in-house success was Edgar G. Ulmer's *Detour,* which wasn't too shabby. They never *quite* rose above their Poverty Row budgets before changing their name to Eagle-Lion Classics; they were sort of the Roger Corman's New World Pictures of their day. Foreign A pictures by day, lurid B movies by night, with some of the country's foremost stylists hard at work on low budget classics. Mann's *T-Men* and the American release of Powell and Pressburger's *The Red Shoes* were big moneymakers. *Black Book* was one of their last productions before shutting down the in-house production apparatus. The studio was sold to United Artists when they realized fighting theater chain monopolies was too costly and annoying. The Eagle-Lion library has very few organic classics, but it is a veritable 'who's who?' of up-and-coming directors, from Ida Lupino to Richard Fleischer. Mann was still the hottest ticket of their stable, which included PRC mainstays like Jean Yarborough, Steve Sekely, Lew Landers, Sam Newfield, Bernard Vorhaus ("Mad Vorhaus" -David Cairns) but Phil Karlson, Stuart Heisler, Roberto Gavaldón and Budd Boetticher were on the make.

In its few years of production, Eagle-Lion made repeated use of cinematographer John Alton for both the ambitious and let's say softball idiocy. Along with the Mann movies he lensed *Canon City,* classic noir B-side *Hollow Triumph* or *The Scar, Red Stallion in the Rockies,* and two by Mad Vorhaus*: Bury Me Dead and The Amazing Mr. X or The Spiritualist.* Alton had lived about six lives before he met Mann. The Hungarian-German Johann Jacob Altmann was born in Sopron, back when Hungary

69

was still a kingdom nestled in an empire, and moved to the US for his collegiate schooling, but that was derailed in the best way when he was taken in as an extra on a movie shooting in New York (the town seems to draw all of *Black Book's* collaborators together in a continuum; place but never time). Fascinated by the production he moved to LA to get more involved and made fast friends with Ernst Lubitsch, who brought him out to Paris to shoot second unit on *The Student Prince of Old Heidelberg*. Alton stayed there but decamped for Argentina with the political climate heating up in Europe in the early 30s. He designed the first Argentine sound studio and started directing and photographing movies at a decent clip so that his reputation meant a little something when he returned triumphant to Los Angeles… only to be saddled with B pictures at Republic Pictures and RKO. You've likely never heard of most of what he got done, I barely knew them, but it's possible you're better versed than I am in 40s Bs. For RKO he shot a couple of *Dr. Christian* movies, with Jean Hersholt as the crusading physician of the title, the first man with two stars on the Hollywood walk of fame, and the man for whom the Jean Hersholt Humanitarian Award was named. This was a prize for actors and artists with a functioning conscience and a spine. Naturally it's only been given out 39 times in 68 years.

For RKO Alton shot the inauspicious likes of *Storm over Lisbon, The Lady and the Monster, Melody for Three, The Trespasser, Winter Wonderland, Wyoming, The Pretender* (by our old friend W. Lee Wilder), and *The Affairs of Jimmy Valentine and Three Faces West* for Mad Vorhaus. After the Mann movies put him on the map in America he quickly became a fixture on the A circuit, though never lost touch with the Bs. He became Vincente Minelli's go-to man at MGM, making ten films together, and photographed Richard Brooks' garish *Brothers Karamazov,* in which the lighting is the only thing worth writing home about. Alton retired after being fired from *Birdman of Alcatraz*, a very troubled prestige production, but he also made a number of ever cheapening Allan Dwan genre films and Joseph H. Lewis' *The Big Combo*, for which he pulled all the tricks he developed with Mann for hiding a film's budget in shadows and fog. It may be Alton's masterpiece, in so far as it's the *most* Alton film in his classic style. *Black Book* of course, a close second.

Before we've even seen the title *Black Book* or *Reign of Terror* (both good titles; if you couldn't tell, I'm having trouble choosing one), we've got billowing smoke and roaring flames, a portent of disaster, of cleansing destruction and the plume of a charred old world (the very same fires that will consume the homestead of Mann's *Devil's Doorway* next year). It opens like *Casablanca* or *Kane* or any one of a dozen 40s films, by situating its audience in its climate of panic and paranoia, where Mann lived most comfortably. The voiceover screams the words "Anarchy! Misery! Murder! Arson! Fear! These are the weapons of dictatorship. One voice is heard. The screech of the guillotine!" The year is 1794. The stakes are set. "In 48 hours, France will have a dictator. In 48 Hours! Unless..." cut to a lone horseman at the bottom of the frame like Robert Mitchum's whistling sadist in *Night of the Hunter.*

Charles D'Aubigny (Robert Cummings) rides to his contact (Wilton Graff) in a resistance network for help, but all he can give him is a time, a place, and a ring (and a gesture…*Tenet*). Faces peer out of the flames, our cast of characters introduced with more screaming elegance than the usual cast list. Cummings, despite many lead roles in Hitchcock films, more or less disappeared from the college-approved roster of stars of post-war American cinema. Like Farley Granger he played desperation well, though unlike the gorgeous Granger, he had an everyman quality that made him a perfect Hitch hero. He came about this character honestly, born to a surgeon who would lose everything in the depression. Cummings ditched a passion for flying airplanes for theatre acting (an early graduate from the Academy of Dramatic Arts, AMDA or SCAMDA as its now referred to by NYU students) because it paid 14 dollars a week and he could no longer afford college. He rode the traveling theatre circuit to LA where King Vidor needed extras who could ride horses. He spent the next five years making thankless Bs for Paramount, who then let his contract expire. He rebounded with Henry Koster's *Three Smart Girls Grow Up,* which wowed critics. "Cummings found himself as an actor," with the picture, wrote Stephen Vagg just a few months ago. From there the hits seemed like they'd never stop. Sam Wood's *Kings Row* and *The Devil and Miss Jones,* and Hitch's *Saboteur,* a movie best known today for everything but Robert Cummings, though he's quite good. Hitch re-used him a few years later, though he's just plain overshadowed by Ray Milland and Grace Kelly in *Dial M For Murder.* Most of us would be. With the films shrinking he turned to TV and wrung another several decades out of his career, dying in 1990. In *Reign of Terror* the first thing someone tells Cummings is that he can blend in in France, which about summarizes his appeal.

The shots of Cummings' approach to France from Austria are riveting. Cummings places himself before a cobwebbed and cracked door, then he steps in and a knife appears before him. Robespierre (Richard Basehart, by now a Mann staple, and one day Gypsy's dream man as she steered the Satellite of Love) kills Danton (Wade

Crosby) before a crowd of fake thousands (Menzies used mirrors to create a liminal space of in-the-round intensity, inventing George Lucas and Roy Andersson; this film was his most effects heavy shoot since *Thief of Baghdad)* and promises more. Robespierre standing before a filmed image of an adoring bloodthirsty mob is the enduring image of the tyrant and the media mogul, who knows that what needs addressing is the simulacra of public opinion, if not the thing itself. It's a fantastic picture of modern sorcery and it's become the truest reflection of the world. Crosby, one of America's dozen or so heirs to Emil Jannings, who never made it to America like his best directors (best not to ask why…). Crosby's first performance was also as Danton in 1938's *Marie Antoinette,* and as here he was also uncredited, though he was uncredited in the bulk of his 95 credits, living long enough to tend bar in *Westworld.* After his sentence is passed, Danton looks directly to camera to issue a warning that in such a climate anyone could be next. Andrzej Wajda would expand Danton's persecution and death into its own film in 1983 with Gerard Depardieu. Its crowning image, of the blood of executed patriots spilling onto sandy ground, is not easily forgotten. One senses Mann would have done the same if he could have gotten away with it. Every second of this film offers an image worth studying and, if you could, moving in and summering there for a semester abroad. And yet the pace demands you never stop to look at anything long, faces clamoring for the frame like Moreau's children in Erle Kenton's *Island of Lost Souls,* murder promised by every interaction.

It's a rare film that makes ordinary coverage seem like a kind of blessed reprieve from the intensity of pure cinema. Arnold Moss is waiting for Basehart's Maximilian ("Don't call me Max!") Robespierre with his deep creaking voice digging into you as his eyes have dug into his face. Though the camera is more or less at rest and the din of the crowd has died down, there are still shadows and framing out of *Caligari* waiting in each reverse angle. "That would make you dictator of France." "Yes…" purrs Basehart. Doves fly into the window of this remote chamber as Basehart feeds and pets them, a beautifully deranged tangent, also connecting it to Hitchcock. This is the longest shot in the scene, so impressed by Basehart's pigeon acting was Mann. Moss, Cummings, Richard Hart, and Jess Barker all need to find the black book in which Robespierre wrote his death list. France will be a different place in each outcome.

Basehart was one of those early Hollywood actors with a rare, artist's attitude toward his work, prefiguring the Brandos and Rylances of the world. He came up as a radio broadcaster for his father's station and transitioned to theatre in the 30s. A few years into his career he was awarded the New York Drama Critics' Circle Award for Most Promising Young Actor and was noticed by film agents and two years later he made his first film, *Repeat Performance* for Eagle-Lion and Alfred Werker, his *He Walked By Night* co-director the next year. Eagle-Lion did him the kindness of premiering the film in Zanesville, Ohio where he was born. There's a sensitivity and openness in his roles after *Reign of Terror.* See it in the part of the reluctantly violent Denno in Sam Fuller's astonishing *Fixed Bayonets!* As the unit thins, he becomes the last man to lead them, and must overcome a crippling anxiety of command, an impotence in the face of violence. One of Fuller's best (though everything is), he is exactly the kind of multifaceted mind and softly featured face he needed to crack open the madness of war and what it does to ordinary men. He went to Italy and made two Fellini films, *La Strada* and *Il Bidone* with fellow expats Anthony Quinn and Broderick Crawford. *La Strada* is the classic, the heaviest hitter of Fellini's 50s, in which an innocent woman (the maestro's blisteringly talented wife Giulietta Masina) must pick between the brute strongman (Quinn) and the more thoughtful trickster, The Fool (Basehart). James Gray would repurpose this dynamic in *The Immigrant* 60 years later.

While in Europe John Huston snatched Basehart up to play Ishmael in *Moby Dick,* ever the innocent, in which his unknowable face beautifully provides us a way into the madness of the central quest and the industry around it. He and Alton would re-unite for *The Brothers Karamazov,* and then he'd skip between oddball projects for the rest of his life. He played Hitler in a biopic by former Eagle-Lion hand Stuart

Heisler and the beastly Sayer of the Law in a *different Island of Dr. Moreau* adaptation, which ought to speak to his fearlessness, his easygoing attitude towards his work. In John Sturges' *The Satan Bug* he reprises his role as Robespierre in all but name, the man who decides who lives and who dies and what civilization will be when he's done with it. His performance has the same simmering placidity, and he walks away with the film, a more thoughtful kind of science fiction picture, a follow-up to Kazan's *Panic in the Streets (on* which *Black Book* writer Philip Yordan did uncredited work on the script), and precursor to Robert Wise's *The Andromeda Strain,* Steven Soderberg's *Contagion* and Rupert Wyatt's *Captive State.* Basehart closed his film career with Hal Ashby's *Being There* as the Soviet ambassador so charmed by Chauncey Gardner, which also served as an epitaph for star Peter Sellers. As usual for the projects Basehart chose, the film was peculiar in its prescience.

"So...you're the *terror* of Strasburg?!" Cummings kills and impersonates a special prosecutor, Duval, whom Basehart will task with finding the book with the names of his enemies, the people who, if they learned were penciled into the book, would rebel against him. Be a shame if it fell into the wrong hands, like those who still believe in the politics of the revolution. Of course, students of history know how this turns out, but they'll either be horrified or stupefied by the way it's told here. Every scene is tense, and every bit of romance and violence charged by tight acres of handsome costuming, which does make one work for a gesture, with sweaty eyes peering from sunken faces and men leaping through windows in topcoats. It's enough to make you check your pulse. Yordan makes this is a noir-ish game of wits, writing dialogue for 1794 that sounds like 1944, and yet it works. After highwaymen try to kill Moss and Cummings in their carriage and the men have to gruesomely dispatch the robbers, Moss says "One thing about Paris... never dull!"

Yordan was one of the most essential scribes of his era. The Chicago born Polish writer who later used himself as a front for blacklisted writers during another reign of terror, that of Senator Joseph McCarty's House Un-American Activities Committee, was an entrepreneur from the get-go (he and Ben Maddow would later squabble over who did what on the films and books for which Yordan allowed the use of his name, the most famous of which are Mann's *Men in War* and *Johnny Guitar*). Like Preston Sturges he started in cosmetics, running a mail order business out of his parent's basement. He studied to become a lawyer but never had the temperament for it and so became an actor then a playwright, and after William Dieterle, The Iron Stove, saw one of his plays he brought him to Hollywood where he did uncredited rewrites on *The Devil and Daniel Webster,* one of Dieterle's best films. Yordan bounced around studios, leaving good to great pictures everywhere he went. He and Cummings opened their own production shingle but it didn't last long, then started his own. He wrote *Drums of the Deep South* for Menzies in 1951, William Wyler's *Detective Story,* modeled after Mann's noirs, Blowing Wild for gifted journeyman Hugo Fregonese, and then re-united with Alton for *The Big Combo*, and Mann for *The Man From Laramie*, both 1955, both magnificent. "Hungarian cyclops" André de Toth's *Day of the Outlaw* (another Cairnsism), which he produced, was his last truly great picture. Then the epics started. *King of Kings, 55 Days at Peking, Battle of the Bulge,* and Mann's own worst films *El Cid* and *Fall of the Roman Empire.* He worked sporadically through the late 60s and 70s before resurfacing with a vengeance in the 1980s, writing erotic thrillers, slasher films and one bigfoot picture. At least one of them, Camilo Vila's *The Unholy* is some kind of classic. Yordan died in 2003, ten years after his official retirement.

Arlene Dahl (one of a few women apparently groomed to be a rival Ingrid Bergman) and Cummings' rekindled romance reads like something out of Chandler. The dialogue is clever, razor sharp, caught between Menzies' bisecting diagonals and standing up like the hair on one's arm. The lack of recognizable faces, all but blending into the wigs and the sets left over from Victor Fleming's *Joan of Arc (starring, who else, Ingrid Bergman),* another film made for producer Walter Wanger, helps the drama go down like wine. Shadows dance in every corner, fire clouds the frame, faces jump into the lens, and everywhere people eavesdropping on this errand of subterfuge. Wanger produced 58 films under his own shingle, 20 or so of them are 5-star films (they include *Stagecoach, Secret Beyond the Door..., Caught, Foreign Correspondent,* and *Invasion of the Body Snatchers. Speaking of which a word about Wanger from my review of Riot in Cell Block 11:* Producer Walter Wanger had wanted to make a movie about prison conditions after serving time for shooting a man in the groin for sniffing around his wife. *Riot on Cell Block 11* opens with a newsreel showing the carnage of prison riots across the country. The photography is as gorgeous and real as the images are terrible and despairing. …maybe a prison riot is the defining image of America, after all… a Law-and-Order country run by criminal scoundrels).

The murder of the special prosecutor Duval is pure slasher: a man falls, a knife rises. Cummings meets Dahl by the shadows cast through venetian blinds, Alton's knowing and gorgeous sop to his noirs. Like many actresses of her generation, early elocution lessons and high school theatre paid off when she was spotted off-

Broadway by a talent scout. After *Reign* she was paired with every kind of leading man – Robert Taylor, Joel McCrea, Van Johnson, Fred Astaire – but she never quite took. The consolation prize was jungle adventure films and then a TV career. Peter Bogdanovich once said of Alida Valli in *The Third Man,* made the same year, that part of why she's so successful in the picture is that she was at her most Ingrid Bergman-esque, which is quite the underhanded compliment (there are many rhymes with *The Third Man* throughout *Black Book,* with its heroine behind enemy lies, and ordinary men shanghaied into webs of conspiracy, coats swishing behind them as they frantically comb European cities for a kernel of truth and with it, proof that the universe has a moral order). If Dahl looks like Bergman, her features are less pointed and "perfect," and her less sharp face collects light even more magically. Bergman's bones betrayed aristocratic breeding, and though she used it well it limited her to a certain kind of angel, fallen or otherwise. You buy Dahl as a revolutionary double agent as you do the princess as which she masquerades. Mann places her in a mirror to illustrate her double life and Cummings' split feelings of betrayal, loss, lust, and admiration.

The innkeeper almost blows Cummings' cover in front of Moss, but he steps into character as the heartless prosecutor, and then he and Moss begin a feline flirtation, trying to out evil each other, which will last all picture long. It becomes rich, sweaty subtext that they pursue each other with more relish than Cummings and Dahl, who are continuously denied a love scene. What's life without a little risk of torture or murder, or…something else… "We're gonna have some great times together, eh Duval?" says Moss with a smirk, twisting the final words of *Casablanca* into a covenant of sadism.

Moss's twisted face, which he always used to great effect as villains under evil goatees, is the film's synecdoche; a preening, haunted ugliness (complimentary) that its star wields like a parade baton. Moss was a Brooklyn boy who worked from radio to speech teacher to stage to Bob Hope bit player to TV mainstay. He was in the first ever production of Stephen Sondheim's *Follies,* which ought to tell you how long and wonderfully strange was his career. *Reign of Terror* was only his fourth film but he's the most memorable actor in the cast. He'd return for Mann's *Border Incident* a few weeks later and close out his career in a 1983 episode of *One Live to Live* that also featured Peter McRobbie, his predecessor, who would play the Fouché role, Representative George Pendleton, in Steven Spielberg's *Lincoln*.

The film of course has no shortage of living (dead) legends. Norman Lloyd, the actor and comedian, plays conspirator Jean-Lambert Tallien, who went from being famous for his range, directing and acting on the stage, starring in dark noir (Losey's *M*, Hitch and Menzies' *Spellbound*) and lighthearted sitcoms, to finally being famous for his incredible age, dying at 106 in 2021, just after he married my friend… you guessed it! David Cairns (hello again David!) to his longtime partner Fiona Watson. Beulah Bondi shows up as a kindly grandmother in the third act, then fresh off Anatole Litvak's *The Snake Pit,* still something like a definitive take on female madness 80 years later. Her career stretched back into the 30s and she died at age 92, having just five years earlier won an Emmy for a guest spot on *The Waltons*. Russ Tamblyn appears, who is still with us at age 90, having gone from childhood hoofer to heartthrob in *West Side Story* to beloved character actor, stealing his every scene in David Lynch's *Twin Peaks,* until Lynch finally relented and stuck him in the woods where he could stand like the force of nature he is, unencumbered by co-stars.

When Cummings and Moss are almost apprehended by counter-revolutionaries Moss shoots one of them in the face and blood sprays all over him, the same effect used in William Friedkin's *To Live and Die in LA,* a similar model of ingenuity on a budget and, like *Black Book,* one of the best films ever made. The torture scene that follows is similarly nervy for the time period – the whole film is bloodier and more explicit than we expect from a film of this vintage – as if we hopped back in time to before the production code was enforced in the mid-30s. Not hard to picture a young Boris Karloff standing watch over these scenes with a scantily clad Myrna Loy in the background. Moss and Cummings eat potatoes on knife point, watching a man get stretched to death on the rack as if they're having cigarettes after sex. Basehart similarly squeezes a lemon idly but firmly as he lays out his plan to retrieve his secret file with Cummings' help. "The people have become a bloodthirsty mob that thrives on human lives…there's only one man that can control this beast." Hungry fellows, these men…

Cummings heads to the Cafe des morts vivants (café of the living dead – great name, unbelievable set design) one of those perfect movie bars like The Blue Parrot in *Casablanca, Dante's* in *The Seventh Victim,* the zeppelin dining car in *Indiana Jones and the Last Crusade,* the Officer's Club in the deeply disappointing *Masters of the Air,* or indeed the luxury bar car in Mann's own *The Tall Target.* A place you never want to leave. Another reason cinema is magic. Shadows dance on the wall, feathered hair touches the ceiling, everyone is dressed for either an execution or New Year's Eve. It's right out of Toulouse-Lautrec, (or perhaps Robert Henri…). Huston would make *Moulin Rouge* about the diminutive painter in the style of his best-known works in 1952 with José Ferrer as the artist, made for British Lion, owned by the Alexander Korda, who had recently been Menzies' boss during his stay in London, and whose brothers, Vincent and Zoltán, had also worked on *The Thief of Bagdad.*

Louis Antoine de Saint-Just (Jess Barker, not to be confused with Fess Parker) introduces himself with a quick identity test for Cummings and then gets back to rabble rousing. Evidently Barker lived just as frivolous a life when he wasn't making *Scarlet Street, Shack Out on 101* and *The Green Berets,* losing paternity suits and dying of liver failure at age 88.

Cummings is attacked again before another meeting with Dahl in a room that looks to have been designed after the bedroom in Queen Christina, starring Greta Garbo and directed by Rouben Mamoulian ("I'm memorizing the room…" my god, what a picture), though of course it was actually used in *Joan of Arc,* a much less sensuous film. The plush curtains and lace drapery and columns and candelabras, you could sink in and sleep. "Just one kiss and four years are wiped out. Life's not that simple…" Cummings suddenly seems stiffer than Dahl, who has loosened like a cravat to really pour it on for her reluctant agent. No pheromone like danger, after all. "Tell me about the women that went with the wine." "They were all called Madelon…" Christ almighty. Yordan earned his salary that day. Her honeyed delivery goes perfectly with the drapes.

Like Polonius, Paul François Jean Nicolas, Vicomte de Barras is hiding behind curtains (Richard Hart – no relation to Richard Basehart – theater actor/journalist/TV regular, and all before his death at age 35 in 1951. Supposedly his illegitimate son dated Leonard Bernstein's wife Felicia Montealegre, so he's a character in the hysterically wrongheaded and very entertaining *Maestro*) of the room waiting for proof that Cummings is Charles D'Aubigny and not Duval, who he's pretending to be. Cummings gets the last laugh on his way out the door. Fouché busts in arrests Barras, only to learn Robespierre has promoted the prosecutor above the law and above Fouché, specifically. He and Barras flee out a window and down a wet cobblestone street lit by torch light, suggesting the work of John Brahm. Water runs down a gutter on the Z axis, ensuring something is always moving. Here the film is like John Ford, *The Informer* or *Long Voyage Home,* where the atmosphere replicates the fog in the heads of his lost heroes.

Cummings heads to prison next, a Menzies anti-paradise of geometric mania, vertical bars everywhere and slumped prisoners below, the lines casting us this way and that. A quick conference with Barras prompts both men to reason that Robespierre never lost his black book, but merely *said* he did as a diversionary tactic to keep his political rivals busy. Robespierre brings Duval's wife to catch him in a lie, but an impostor (Georgette Windsor, whose only other movie was Richard Whorf's *Luxury Liner*) beats the genuine article (Mary Currier, who stayed on set after *Joan of Arc,* making her last film appearance before retiring) to the jail. Madelon carts him off seconds before the ruse is discovered. Knowing he beat

Robespierre back to his library, D'Aubigny passes a bakery that looks like a pre-code harem, each dough beater shirtless and tired. Menzies puts rifles, more vertical lines, every few inches in Robespierre's study down a spiral staircase, finding a way to make every inch of the set graphically pleasing. A guard dog barks at Cummings. "Greetings…patriot…" He disarms the canine with affection, and then does the same to Fouché, whose massive beak enters the frame as a colossal shadow on the wall. They promise each other privilege and safety in the new France if either ends up on top, and get to work looking for the book in "Max's" study. The study is in complete darkness but for Max's desk, an eerie effect that wouldn't be out of place in a Disney cartoon of the same vintage. The study has about a thousand black books (more lines). Now to find the right one…

If *Black Book* has meaningful precedent beyond the feel, the satanic vibe of pre-code horror and caper films, it's the work of Val Lewton, the producer wunderkind who proved so invaluable to David O. Selznick as his assistant that he was put in charge of his own horror unit at RKO. There Lewton reinvented the horror picture, prizing atmosphere over monsters and mad science. *Cat People,* the unit's coming out party movie, was even filmed on the leftover sets, Lewton's from *The Magnificent Ambersons,* another collection of shadows and leering mugs, just like *Black Book.* Jacques Tourneur, its director, was a kind of gentle rival figure to Mann, both working miracles on a pauper's pittance for major minors. Tourneur had come from shorts and thankless detective movies, just a step above serials, for Republic Pictures, before Lewton rescued him and made something special out of the bookish Frenchman. *Out of the Past* gamely kept company with Mann's best films noir, while *Canyon Passage* anticipates Mann's Jimmy Stewart westerns. *Circle of Danger* was an Eagle-Lion Classics production just after Mann and Alton stopped working for them.

From my patreon writing on Tourneur's movies: Jacques Tourneur was born wealthy to a director father and actress mother, but the prosperity wasn't a guarantee so much as a glimpse into a potential future. He got a job editing two-minute films throughout the twenties while his father made a name for himself as an internationally regarded talent (the pair briefly emigrated to Hollywood in the teens but returned before too long), but he had the poor fortune of working between two wars; a time to be easily foreshadowed by other talents and by history.

Tourneur said farewell to his European home once more to see if opportunity might be kinder to him in the states away from the sound of cannons loading and hands wringing, leaving three *very* difficult-to-find features behind him. He started making 10-minute historical shorts for MGM (the young Tourneur was almost never seen without a literary classic under his arm, both a posture and a genuine affectation) and shooting second unit for David O. Selznick, whom he met in 1935, the same year he married his wife Christiane, before he finally moved to feature length movies at the end of the 30s. The Walter Pigeon-starring Nick Carter movies, based on a popular radio program, were hardly a high risk venture. More a matter of putting the director somewhere he couldn't do too much harm (Tourneur also returned for the sequel

Phantom Raiders). His wife always nagged him about money until the day he got his first real paycheck at MGM for directing. He came home and spread the money across her body while she slept. Looks like he was here to stay.

He reinvented himself, Val Lewton, fright films, and the 20th century with *Cat People.* There are no casual *Cat People* fans and by extension very few casual Jacques Tourneur or Val Lewton fans. It is possible to admit that all of their films were not created equally but Tourneur's heyday is essentially unequaled for mood and ingenuity on a tight budget, except by Man. Tourneur and Lewton invented a certain *kind* of low budget movie out of whole cloth when they unleashed this mysterious little number on unsuspecting audiences in 1942. Lewton was the rare producer that people (well...*film* people) loved as much as his product because he lost sleep making sure the movies were *good* rather than expensive or properly scaled. He made the careers of his three upstart directors, Tourneur, Mark Robson (who edited Cat People), and Robert Wise (who betrayed Orson Welles and then Lewton) and nearly gave one to Hugo Fregonese; if only people actually *enjoyed Apache Drums* at the time of its release. Stanley Kramer was inspired to make movies because of Lewton and the social consciousness and artistic aspirations flooding both his horror films and his problem pictures *(*like *Mademoiselle Fifi,* Lewton's own *Black Book*, a romantic period piece made for pennies*)*. Tourneur stayed an underdog, however, never rising to Robson and Wise's mediocre but profitable highs but exacting a greater degree of control in his smaller wheelhouse.

His last film was the *very* cheap Edgar Allen Poe adaptation *City In The Sea* or *War-Gods of the Deep*. The film's threadbare and a little dull in stretches, but I can think of no better circumstances under which Tourneur might have said goodbye to his artform. Based on a classic but crafted from whole cloth, the man with a book ever under his arm, the man who created nightmares from shadows and suggestions. A movie that had no right to exist, and certainly no right to be so beguiling. He never made *War and Peace*. Nor *Bleak House*. He was never allowed to be a maker of the epics he so prized, that his father made before disappearing. He was destined to shadows. And in shadow he made symphonies.

And when, amid no earthly moans, Down, down that town shall settle hence, Hell, rising from a thousand thrones, Shall do it reverence...

Cat People's creation is mythologized by Vincente Minnelli in *The Bad and the Beautiful,* which would be one of the great acts of love one director ever gave another, except of course the Lewton figure in that film is painted as an opportunist cad who sold his director out at the first sign of trouble, when the opposite was true. Lewton himself got sold down the river by Robson and Wise who cut him out of a deal to start their own studio together (the stress of which didn't help his frail constitution; he died of a series of heart attacks a few years later). History, winners. As ever, as ever, as ever. The gist of it is that Lewton was given a title and a release date and, terribly embarrassed by the assignment, pulled off one of the greatest feats of producorial subterfuge in American cinema. He hired magnificent queer screenwriter DeWitt Bodeen and asked Tourneur to dig into the stores of talent he'd been insufficiently encouraged to pursue as an MGM gopher. Suitably Tourneur, the man with the ever present Russian novel on his person while walking the backlot, opens with a quote from a fake volume called *The Anatomy of Atavism*, written by the spine-tinglingly oily psychiatrist heel of the picture, Tom Conway's Dr. Louis Judd. It reads: "*Even as fog continues to lie in the valleys, so does ancient sin cling to the low places, the depressions in the world consciousness.*" This is both a joke about the film's pretenses towards beating its birth right (it's a *real* movie with *real* source, you see) but also a way to trick the audience into gearing up for something more worldly and sensitive than its lurid title implied.

Martin Scorsese has dug deep into Lewton's repurposing of his European heritage in his fiction and non. Lewton's history was his sketchbook and the tortured Serbian woman at *Cat People's* heart both a spin of the Yalta born producer's experiences as an immigrant who can't go home, a tribute to his feisty aunt, the actress Alla Nazimova, and Bodeen's as a gay man in a very cruel world of straights unwilling to bend their conception of reality to include him in it. When we meet Irina Dubrovna (Simone Simon, whose beautifully unpolished and unforgettably child-like performance is one of the best in horror) she's sketching too. She's drawing the central park zoo's panther, whose feminine screaming she says she hates, because, it is everything she is and is not. She's behind bars no one can see, and it's only her skin that keeps her out among people. As everyone by now must know: when Irena gets sexually aroused she turns into a panther and goes on nocturnal missions of death and defilement. When she marries engineer Oliver Reed (Kent Smith - a pre-modern Bill Irwin) she can't consummate their marriage out of fear she'll paint the walls with this milquetoast fellow's blood. As Oliver drifts towards his Hawksian co-worker Alice (Jane Randolph), Irene seeks Judd's counsel, and he suggests maybe his sexually assaulting her might cure her of her perceived puritanism. He's more right and wrong than he knows.

Bodeen and Lewton making Irena a castaway from Serbia allowed them and Tourneur to mold the expectations of their audience. By now, between the Germany of *Frankenstein,* the Wales of *The Wolf Man,* the Romania of *Dracula* and the Hungary of *The Black Cat,* American audiences had come to associate European countries with far-away evil and unearthly creation (this mirrored America's perception of the rise of Fascism as a European phenomenon; ignoring that their own country concealed a rotting core that would turn to the same tenets if pushed even a little in anything resembling an uncomfortable direction). Irena was still a pretty bold spin on the Universal monsters and the vampire mythos after the likes of *The Bride of Frankenstein* and *Dracula's Daughter.* The sexual content of the likes of *Dracula* and *Bride* are on the surface, of course, but so remote and strange that not even a certified kook like James Whale let us think about the creature and his bride consummating their marriage for *too* long. In *Cat People* Irena won't even let Oliver kiss her; the implications are staggering.

Though the film is wonderfully frightening and erotically outrageous, it's the princess's naivete of Simon's performance that keeps all of that in check. Despite Simon showing up in William Dieterle's *All That Money Can Buy* or *The Devil and Daniel Webster* as sexual temptation incarnate, here you *want* her to stay virginal, both for her sake and ours. To think of such an innocent succumbing to her urges is designed to upset an audience both in the war years and today where puritanism is making a comeback. If she weren't so lovable, maybe the comparatively liberated Alice, or the poised and deadly looking Serbian (Elizabeth Russell) who offers Irena companionship on her wedding night, would threaten to unleash a different thing indeed. Irena's heartbreak at her own condition is what unsettles and breaks our heart. When she kills a bird, a gift from her loving, devoted, and *frustrated* husband, like a cartoon cat, her sorrow at discovering that she has the power to take life reverberates through your whole body. Why is this dreadful thing happening to such a lovely person?

Though of course for every lovely thing she does that backfires she discovers untapped stores of malicious sadism lying dormant in her, like the cat that wants to crawl its way out. She attacks Judd after goading him into trying to make good on his promises to make her give up her fantasy through sexual release, and she stalks Alice to maintain the status quo (she's like Royal Tenenbaum, gliding through New York penthouses hoping nothing will change for the worst). The attack on Judd is not merely because of his own predation but because he's spent the lion's share of his screen time convincing Irena that she's invented her problem despite what her body and her mind tell her. More so than many of the shapeshifting narratives of the first half of the 20th century, *Cat People's* message of bodily autonomy is very clearly designed (think Tourneur's collection of classic novels) to outlast the moment, to speak to people everywhere whose bodies are telling them something that society won't. "Whatever's in me, it's hemmed in, it's kept harmless... if I'm happy." But how often are we happy? How often do we feel like keeping this *thing* (our true identity) inside of us is the right decision.

Cat People is one of the first movies in America to suggest that what's being villainized is something natural (hereditary or possibly genetic) that no one else can understand. Frankenstein's monster was made. Count Dracula is defined by lust and charisma, his "condition" isn't made clear in his first movies. Dr. Jekyll and Mr. Hyde are separated by scientific advances, without which Jekyll would never have understood what he was keeping at bay. Irena, the one without a literary source, is the one who understands that there's more to her than what people see and can understand. When she embraces it, the world around her falls apart. Like a Welles hero she is the engine of her own destruction, but unlike a Welles hero, she *truly* cannot help that this is who she is because you cannot fight your body and your soul at once. Nor should you. She may not want to admit she's a panther, but she's known it longer than her new husband, his mistress, and her psychologist understand. They've met a person and discovered a problem. Irena has had an understanding of herself most of her whole life. The last line of the film? "She never lied to us."

With all this richness of subtext, some of it waiting like Irena for a more empathetic moment in history (relatively speaking, he says, checking the news of the day) the film is still perhaps most justifiably remembered for its innovations in horror technique. It invented the jump scare by most accounts (which Lewton and his team called a "bus" when designing new ones because the first one involved the false anticipation of a murder while waiting for one) and relied heavily on suggestion over demonstration. Partly this was an idea born of empty pockets but also it was smarter than trying to outdo the prosthetics found on Boris Karloff and both Lon Chaneys for sheer shock value. What if you just convinced the audience that there was a hungry jungle cat waiting for you in every shadow? Wouldn't *that* make you lose sleep? It worked and so the Lewton horror movies, 9 in all, would get you to believe something before they ever had to show it to you. Creeping paranoia and a menacing atmosphere would do half the work and then the sight of the simplest, most upsetting thing would seal the deal. When I made my second horror film, *Eyam,* I leaned heavily on Lewton's idea of a horror movie. From *Cat*

People came the empty hallways at night and the notion that something out there in the dark wanted to harm you. From *I Walked With a Zombie,* the notion of unrequited love with an interloper in a faraway place stalked by the living dead. From *The Leopard Man,* women keeping a fanged evil just on the other side of the door at bay. From *The Seventh Victim,* the idea of suicide as the only salvation from the curse of the self. From *Ghost Ship* a crew of doomed men on a voyage towards death. From *Curse of the Cat People,* the pent-up emotion of the neglected turning malevolent. *From Isle of the Dead,* fear of death to a pestilence. From *The Body Snatcher,* the feeling of imprisonment in a place designed to help the imperiled, held hostage by people who know you best. From *Bedlam* the Quaker heroine - although I was raised Quaker so let's call that one a draw. Almost a hundred years after Lewton reinvented the horror movie and he's still writing my road map."

Next came *I Walked With A Zombie.* Myself again: "I walked with a zombie...seems a funny thing to say." Lewton and Tourneur, after just one picture, had the gentrification of ghouls down to a science, though they had help that usually goes uncredited - indeed the writing credit does not, as was custom in these days, immediately precede producer and director's names. Our writers are Curt Siodmak, Robert's "idiot brother" to quote David once again (and yes, he did make *Bride of the Gorilla* and *Love Slaves of the Amazon,* even if he also co-directed *People on Sunday*), and the still preposterously unheralded Ardel Wray, who like composer Roy Webb, calypso singer Sir Lancelot, and editor-turned director Mark Robson was an intrinsic member of the Val Lewton stock company of interpreters. She wrote the next three Lewton pictures, then vanished, torn up over Lewton's death, re-emerging to write TV in the 1960s. She'd been raised by her grandfather, humanitarian mogul B.F. Brisac - who famously traveled post-earthquake San Francisco with money and a pistol fulfilling insurance claims to newly jobless locals while warding off looters. Her mother abandoned her with a Christian Scientist businessman to go write dialogue for Thomas Ince. Wray followed her mother to Hollywood after deciding not to be an actress or a model. Freshly divorced for a second time, she turned up at RKO, rumors of a fling with Dalton Trumbo in her background - which may have been her ticket to Lewton. Robson had worked at Trumbo's favourite bakery in the early 30s.

Curt turned in a draft of *I Walked With a Zombie* that Lewton found insufficiently atmospheric; Curt's *Wolfman* script explains both why Lewton was unsatisfied with his first draft and what he learned from his time in the RKO story department. Inez Wallace, a now mostly forgotten journalist who specialized in sensational travel stories, had been to Haiti in search of the truth of zombies like Zora Neale Hurston before her, and came back with a tabloid style account of her encounters with the undead in the country's interior; they read not dissimilarly to the opening of *White Zombie,* this movie's only real forebearer. One account of Lewton encountering Wallace's tale has Lewton taken with the hints of Charlotte Brontë in her telling, but the Wallace story might as well be a report from the World's Fair or a factory in desperate need of regulation; there's hardly any romance at all. I think it's far more likely that Wray or Lewton saw the potential for such a marriage and hammered it out. Regardless Tourneur understood what both writers were asking of him and delivered a film of even more potent atmosphere than *Cat People*. Within minutes we're on the boat to the Caribbean listening to the low and somber humming of the shipmen; transported completely.

By reframing the sensational source as an epistolary account of a naive woman's encounter with not just the wider world but with its darkest forces and unknowable supernatural happenings, they've refused the obviousness of a white woman heading into colonial subjects to do good, as Brooke Dubek might frame it, though not so much that the film's zombie, Darby Jones, was paid substantially less than his white co-stars for his three days of work. Francis Dee's Betsy Connell is a nurse fresh from the academy (shades of Wray's own background are found heavily made-up in the movies she wrote for RKO) whose first assignment is a plantation on the fictitious Saint Sebastian Island. The image of the publicly pierced body will recur throughout the film, and indeed the sexualization of horror was something of a Lewtonian specialty. Tom Conway's Paul Holland is her guide ("quite the Byronic character...") and he's introduced reading young Betsy's mind. His half-brother, James Ellison's Wesley Rand, fell in love with Paul's wife Jessica (Christine Gordon) and just before they could leave together she became ill with some horrible fever that's left her catatonic, hence the need for a nurse. She's the classic madwoman in the attic, codified by Sandra Gilbert and Susan Gubar in novels like *Jane Eyre*. She's introduced as a perfect white figure in a black void, malevolent in her unreachable stupor. As in the previous year's *Casablanca* a lot of ground is covered in public squares, with Betsy hearing Sir Lancelot singing about the dishonor of the Holland/Rand household in a jaunty little tune used to taunt the whites who still lord their power over the island, even though it's quite thoroughly diminished. That song would later end up as a theme for a gossipy English radio broadcast whenever the royals would embarrass themselves. "Shame dishonor for the family…"

Tourneur films this colonial passion play with his tremendous chiaroscuro lighting and shifty compositional sense. Shadows and silhouettes travel with the shambling speed of Darby Jones' zombie walk. Torch light and eerie studio lighting meet in the false studio night sky. He reveals things, whether jealous lovers or undead messengers, hiding in perfect darkness. Tourneur's framing of Jones' is at once the film's greatest strength and weakness - it so exquisite and frightening a set of images that cannot help but other the man completely. Jones' Carrefour guards the vodou houngan (Martin Wilkins) and his disciples from interference and a bust of Saint Sebastian, the figurehead of the first slave ship that christened the island, guards the Holland's homestead. The battle lines well drawn. Jones performance manages to exude such melancholy in just a few moments of screentime with no dialogue and bulging prosthetic eyes over his own, it's a shame no one ever figured out what else to do with him (he reprised the part in the dreadful *Zombies on Broadway*). The film *is* a patch on the bulk of horror of this vintage dealing with black characters or blackness generally speaking, but the calculous is still unfair. Comparisons are always bound to make something superior when an honest accounting wouldn't land you there. Still, Miriam Bale called it one of the greatest American films of all time. Manny Farber agreed, and so do I.

At the John and Francis Ford Festival in Portland Maine the weekend of August 20th, 2023, I once more heard from people as esteemed and intelligent as Joseph McBride and Loren Schoenberg wave away the racism inherent in John Ford films as progressive or, at bottom, forgivable. To me it's a fool's errand to treat films of this vintage as anything but, at best, forward *looking*. You won't find true progressivism in Hollywood because it wasn't allowed and nobody thought it was profitable. Lewton only got away with his version of it because he was working in a B picture unit and was so well-liked by David O. Selznick. Sort of an Abraham Lincoln of genre, trying his best and getting it wrong all the time. His black characters remain servants and butlers, though they're allowed a good deal higher a ration of dignity than Ford allowed Stepin Fetchit or, to use McBride's own counter example, the black characters in Frank Capra movies (I confess no expertise on Capra, though Bedford Falls *is* an integrated community). The transgressive thing in *I Walked with a Zombie* is that though the black characters who work for the Holland plantation are undoubtedly in his employ and are stuck replaying the hideous legacy of colonialism in the Caribbean, they've found a way to subvert their role in the drama. They're the ones controlling the mesmerized Jessica Holland, the ones who get to use their culture to mock the distended slaver mindset that still troubles the men in the big house. Holland knows slavery's a crucible and a crime, but he still plays his role on the island and Lewton, Tourneur, and Wray play knowingly with the contradictions.

Saint Sebastian is so outwardly beautiful, so inwardly ugly, burning with hatred born of a history of violence, people free only because the white masters cannot fully understand their Vodou culture (though Paul's mother [Edith Barrett] tries in order to get them to comply with healthier standards - still patronizing in their best humanitarian disguise), represented by the constant drumming on the soundtrack in direct combat with Paul Holland's staccato and distracted piano playing. One of these groups has community, togetherness, a way of life that makes sense to them. The other are trudging through a parody of opulence that has long since ossified. "I'm afraid it's not that frightening," says Paul of the Vodou rituals. He's right. How can anything on Saint Sebastian be frightening when it's become so normalized that not even the living dead seem an affront to the status quo? "You can't look at him and lead him at the same time," says Francis Dee of a horse, but it's clear what she and Wray mean by this innocent little turn of phrase. Lewton, Wray, and Tourneur offer something that, at last, does seem faintly progressive: if the living won't do the right thing, the dead have a way of forcing their hand. They'll tell your story one way or the other.

Then Tourneur's final picture for Lewton, *The Leopard Man*. To the sound of insistent, almost *menacing* castanets, the camera creeps down a corridor, finding the author of the noise, then jackknifing right to find the dancer's rival. Kiki and Clo-Clo are competing for the attention of a nightclub audience and its owner, Jerry Manning. Manning knows he's got a good thing on his hands with their rivalry and has found the perfect tool to turn it into box office: a leopard on a leash. Be a shame if he got loose, wouldn't it? This is the thrust of Cornell Woolrich's novel *Black Alibi* and its adaptation by Ardel Wray, Jacques Tourneur, and Val Lewton, the fiendishly good *The Leopard Man*.

The first camera movement isn't on paper anything special; the camera moves down a hall slowly, then quickly, then *just* as quickly changes direction. It's the malevolent purpose of the dolly that's so stunning. It's not quite killer POV-cam (with which *Black Book* also flirts), but that's the idea, but more importantly it's the movie in a single maneuver. We're looking at something until someone steals our attention away, from castanets to irate banging on the wall. Not only is rivalry on stage the subject, it's also a movie ultimately about sleight of hand. Look this way, not that way, and miss the big picture. Miss what's right in front of you.

Mononymous Margo (though in actuality: María Marguerita Guadalupe Teresa Estela Bolado Castilla y O'Donnell) learned to dance with Eduardo Cansino (Rita Hayworth's dad) and then performed with her uncle Xavier Cugat. This led to a film career and a marriage to Eddie Albert and just as quickly to their blacklisting when she was spotted at a communist rally in defiance of Generalissimo Francisco Franco (later Mann's benefactor). Albert managed a second act, but Margo wasn't that lucky, nor that interested. She founded a cultural education and arts center in LA that's still there and her dresses were put on display at the Natural History Museum of LA County. On the stage and off, even now that she's gone, she always commanded a room. Clo-Clo is the film role for which she's best remembered. Her superb castanet playing, her deep mellifluous voice, her lithe movement, she's more leopard than leopard. She should have won an Oscar for the way she smokes a cigarette.

Wray's collection of catty women here is one of her finest casts of characters (Edward Dein wrote some of the dialogue, 15 years before making *Curse of the Undead,* the first American horror western) from Clo-Clo and Kiki (Jean Brooks) to the jaded fortune teller (Isabell Jewell, so tired she's dreaming), to the over-eager cigarette girl (Ariel Heath) to the spoiled heiress (Jacqueline deWit) to say nothing of a bit part for Finnish violinist Tuulikki Paananen as an ailing diva. "I must go to the cemetery, it's my birthday!" Then there's the skittish little girl who cries wolf. She complains too long to her mother about going out to do chores that when she starts screaming to be let in the house because she's being murdered, mom doesn't believe her and is too late to save her. Lewton had gone dark before but killing a pre-adolescent? That was as vicious a thing as you'd find in a movie of this vintage. Somehow this savage killing of an innocent flew beneath the radar of the production code like the little girl's blood seeping under the locked door. Shocking, even now.

Reviews at the time were unkind and today *The Leopard Man* is one of the least discussed of the Lewton horrors, along with *The Ghost Ship,* but its atmosphere is dreadful and its little world of hucksters and dreamers a nastily ingratiating place to be (rather like *Black Book's*), more so than *Cat People's* upper east side or *I Walked with a Zombie's* haunted plantation. The jump scares penetrate the thick atmosphere much more aggressively, as well, from a train distracting from two evil eyes under a bridge (a chilling sight indeed) to a car's engine scaring a girl trapped in a graveyard on her birthday. You can sense the foundations of *Nightmare Alley* and breathe the fumes of *Freaks* in this quick and cheap little number (it was shot in a month and released two months later and even recycled the cat from *Cat People!*). Mario Bava and William Friedkin were both transfixed by it, and indeed it's tough to imagine their cinematic torment of young women without its transgressions. Anyone could be guilty in this one, almost everyone is of something or other. It's a little ant colony of small-time crime and petty schemes. "Sure I'm a gold digger! Why not!?" It's a cutthroat little movie, one of the earliest slasher films where mothers and daughters alike are butchered, strivers get mutilated for their ambition, a place with no heroes.

Lewton followed these up with *The Ghost Ship, Curse of the Cat People, Isle of the Dead, The Seventh Victim, Bedlam,* and *The Body Snatcher.* Between the nine that's three period pieces, with an eye for beauty and grotesquerie every bit as specific as Mann's on *Black Book.* Add to the cauldron the casual murders in *Leopard Man,* the warped authority figures of *Isle of the Dead, The Ghost Ship,* and *Bedlam,* the cackling sadists of *Cat People, The Seventh Victim,* and *The Body Snatcher* and you've got a combined effect every bit as forward thinking in its vision of horror as *Black Book.* And then of course there are the scares and the misdirection. Lewton's "bus" scare finds its way into *Black Book* as Fouché and D'Aubigny Robespierre's study. The sound of an approaching footfall anticipates not a soldier or Max himself, but the faithful hound dog. Both men exhale, relieved. And just when we've settled into a false sense of safety, Fouché hears his own name in the Black Book's index of traitors and lunges at D'Aubigny with a knife he sees in shadow on the pages of the book, a replay of the shadow of his face a few moments ago (you can see Bava and Dario Argento studying movies like this). It is the shadow, the double of this man, always playing both sides, that impresses more than the hollow man himself. Look for his like again in Robert Preston in *The Last Frontier, Ralph Meeker* in *The Naked Spur,* and if you're feeling generous Christopher Plummer in *Fall of the Roman Empire*.

D'Aubigny's struggle to escape from Robespierre's library and bakery ends in a hail of gunfire and it's shocking how tactile the impacts are. You see little hints of Sam Peckinpah in the way a pistol destroys a table thrown at a lieutenant. There's more beautiful Disney cartoon form in the image of a white-hot spear pulled from a fireplace and used to menace all and sundry so D'Aubigny can finally get away. He goes to a market to meet up with a contact using coded language. His contacts stand on opposite sides of the frame, Cummings in the middle, to ensure even a scene a few seconds long does not let the eye down. Madelon and D'Aubigny flee to a country inn disguised as farmers. Beulah Bondi runs the inn. Peter Bogdanovich went on a riff about Bondi for a Criterion Collection spot about Leo McCarey's five star, six hankie *Make Way for Tomorrow* about fifteen years ago in which he recounts a conversation with Orson Welles. "Shame she only made one good picture…" said the younger man, clearly forgetting she made this. "Well, you only need one." Keep the lesson, forget what produced it. In criticism and in life.

Soldiers arrive at the inn sending Cummings and Dahl into the most beautiful barn set of all time and sending Bondi into a snit ("Swine" "What's that?" "Some more wine?"). She notices the black book, left behind in the haste to flee, on the bed where Saint-Juste sleeps. She attempts over and over to snatch it away but fails. Bondi's grandchildren are utilized to distract Saint-Juste's gun hands, while Cummings steals a horse and Dahl steals the book. Rear projection creates distance in a forest between the lovers and their pursuers, but Mann ingeniously hides the screen behind trees on the set to aid the illusion. This has to be one of the only instances of this technique where the camera is pointed at a downward diagonal from a treetop. Dahl is captured and brought to Robespierre's office for torture while our three villains, Fouché, Saint-Juste, and Max watch, stifling their glee at the proceedings. The image of Dahl being lowered from the ceiling, ropes around her wrists, reminds one of the torture dungeon montage in Sternberg's *Scarlet Empress*, another film of court intrigue and well-lit women.

Barras is brought before Robespierre, vulture-like on a dais overlooked by the false rear projected crowds; it's a better effect than the real thing would have been. D'Aubigny has already handed The Black Book to the audience and seeing the names for themselves as Robespierre uselessly babbles about France's need for a dictator and that dictator's need to sacrifice people for the good of the nation, start to get very angry indeed. Ken Russell's *The Devils* will pick up this scene and ride it into Valhalla, complimenting its taut form with writhing nuns and shirtless witchfinders. The malcontent faces once more spring at the camera voicing their displeasure. They come for Robespierre, whom Fouché orders shot in the face; in reality Robespierre killed himself in front of the assembled. Ridley Scott would stage this accurately in his *Napoleon* in 2023, adding more blood and attendant confusion where Mann could only shock us with flashes of it all. It is Napoleon who strides onto the scene in the film's final seconds, promising more death and mayhem to come. They wrap up Robespierre's mouth in bloody cloth like a Universal monster and drag him off. From the formal address to the attendant party after Robespierre's bloody demise, shades of Michael Cimino's *Heaven's Gate,* perhaps the last word on bloody historical rebellion, one of the last modernist pictures with real bravery to come out of the studio system, hit the walls. And to add insult to injury the bleeding Robespierre is marched to the guillotine and beheaded. "He planned on leaving statues of himself. All he leaves behind is…stale bread."

There's a most grim implication to the bearded soldier, wine leaking onto the floor from a discarded skin, who has secreted Madelon behind Robespierre's bookshelf. That's a long time to keep a woman to yourself. I don't wanna know what he did to kill time. D'Aubigny burns the building down and tears open the passage with a spear, like one of the Warriors in Cy Endfield's 1962 *Zulu,* attacking the hospital wing, full of malingerers and dying drunken firebrands. Cummings and Dahl walk together out of the fire and into the street. Order restored...for a couple of minutes. Mann made great films before and after this, but nothing, not even stunning companion piece *The Tall Target,* quite has its nerve, its invention, its style.

Border Incident – 1949

Mann returned from the antiquated netherworld of *Reign of Terror* to his procedurals with the blistering *Border Incident,* which opens with a gorgeous set of helicopter shots of the Southwest before landing on a claustrophobic shot of faces and arms behind two layers of chain-link fence, the diagonals of farmland becoming that of imprisonment and immiseration. Within seconds the thesis. Opportunity for some, backbreaking labor for others. Food for you, life and death for them. André Previn's incredible, tremulous, hugely exciting score then takes us to the silky sands of the borderlands, where illegal workers struggle to get across, while John Alton's camera alternately waits for their faces to collide with him or watches from a safe distance as murderers and pirates prepare to strip these poor bastards of their last possessions and dump their bodies in quicksand. Martin Garralaga, Harry Antrim, Ricardo Montalban, and George Murphy get sent from Washington and Mexico City, respectively, to put an end to the murder on the border. Montalban almost never got to play a Mexican, because he, like Anthony Quinn, was tasked with playing whatever ethnicity the A pictures needed. By the time they were A picture stars, Hollywood had little need of them except as scenery chewing anti-heroes of unimportant ethnicity.

This was Mann's first major studio production (Alton's too), and MGM let him do whatever he wanted, figuring he'd been making pretty good money for the little guys across town. Though of course they had no idea what to do with the film when Mann turned it in - it lost money, but it's incredible. He manages to add the kind of black comic edge of B. Traven's *Treasure of the Sierra Madre* to his usual noir template. Montalban goes undercover as a bracero to ferret out the killers, Murphy as a crooked immigration fixer. It doesn't take long before the carefully laid plans fall apart, violently. There's a bracing death scene that still takes one off guard in 2024. The camera gets as close to the face of death before the machinery of capitalism rends the flesh of a scared man off screen, but you'll feel it anyway. The film is subtle in all things and then there will be sudden onslaughts of symbolism and the sweaty faces of its characters moments before meeting them.

The cast also includes Arnold Moss and Charles McGraw, back from *Black Book,* José Torvay, John Ridgely, Arthur Hunnicutt, Howard Da Silva, James Mitchell, Sig Ruman, Robert Cabal, Harry Antrim, and Alfonso Bedoya - a lot of white guys play Mexicans but the fact that the film centers on Montalban does count for something, to say nothing of giving the film the heft of his incredible, theatrical work. The great character faces blend in with the production design, by now a Mann trademark. The emphasis on the drama of spaces rather than plot gives the film a unique feel, much less hyped up than *Reign of Terror,* much less business minded than *T-Men.* The beautiful musical underpinning and lengthy, loaded silences together give the film the feel of a western like the following year's *Wagon Master.* You see sand blow from under the wheels of trucks for yards along placid landscape shots and hear little but the tired bellow of the engine. In the final act it becomes a slithering tale of espionage as our heroes slink about in canyons or on ill-gotten property. Every so often you feel a low budget horror film breaking out from the confines of the studio message thriller. It's still basically unlike any film of the time - Mexican heroes who outlive the white savior, capitalist thugs crucified by their own knives, and long passages of unbearably tense quiet. Any given five minutes will tell you why MGM didn't know what Mann had handed them. But they'll also remind you why he was one of the best directors of his era.

Side Street – 1949

"You like poetry, kid?" I saw *Side Street* at Chicago's Music Box Theatre for the annual Noir City programming festival and was *very* excited to see Mann on 35mm, even if it wasn't shot by John Alton. Mann was enticed to MGM by Sam Zimbalist and evidently Alton wasn't included in the bargain. He gave him Joseph Ruttenberg instead, and well yeah, I guess he's as good as you were going to get if Alton or James Wong Howe weren't around, right? Just look at these credits! *Fury, Philadelphia Story, A Day At The Races, The Women, Gaslight, Mrs. Miniver...* you seeing the problem yet? Great films, great directors, none of them known for their visual style not already a feature of their director (Ok, yes, I'm just talking about Fritz Lang). He was a capable photographer of drama...he wasn't a voyager and discoverer. He was a first mate. He wasn't John Alton. Explains why *Side Street* was rather blown off the screen by Jean Negulesco's *Deep Valley* on the double bill that day at Noir City, true noir phantasmagoria, but there's still great stuff here. The directness entrances. "Let it lay," says a gangster with his foot on two hundred dropped dollars. The silence deafens, the blood runs cold. "Havana, Miami...by way of the East River." A gangster's girl is picked up by a trawler right as a mailman gets the idea to rob that gangster. Coincidence and bad luck. The stuff that dreams are made of.

Paul Kelly starts us off with more of Mann's by-now trademark proto-*Dragnet* narration. "The name's ~~Friday~~ Captain Walter Anderson." He describes the crimes and times of New York ("Maybe this fellow wants to recapture his lost youth," he says. Speak for yourself, pal) before landing on Farley Granger's starry-eyed lover (he seldom played anything but lovers, starry or otherwise; too pretty for much else) who wants a mink for pregnant wife Cathy O'Donnell. Writer Sydney Boehm (later Lang's *The Big Heat,* a couple of Fregoneses, *Hell on Frisco Bay*, and the perfectly named *A Nice Little Bank That Should Be Robbed*, which I now must see even if it *is* a Mickey Rooney comedy) has clearly seen Jules Dassin's *The Naked City* from the year before, the most docurealistic of the 40s films noir, also New York-set, also reliant on her architecture. The narrator seems afraid of silence, ruining great moments like Granger first attempting to break into a filing cabinet. He knows he's done the wrong thing because his mail bag, the albatross of his low-class life, slips around his hands as he struggles. Still crazed by ambition he grabs a fire ax and tries again. I had already seen this and the sight of Granger's eyes bugging as he grabs the thing shocked me all over again.

The inevitability of the outcome and the heel dragging to get there is what bothers me about a film like *Side Street* and indeed *Side Street* in particular. Mann frames it all wonderfully (the blocking is busily divine; a panting Pekingese with a smushed up face joins a line-up of cops and fits right in) and the drama's of course well played but it's just no fun watching nice people squirm while bad people close in. Especially when they're as expressive as Granger and O'Donnell. You hurt with them in every tendon and joint. And watching the sweaty man lurch from place to place, hellhounds on his trail… It's good cinema, I suppose, must be, but it's just not much *fun*. The guy gets the absolute *shit* kicked out of him. It's like *Good Time* but trade Robert Pattinson for Granger. Early method theatrics making their way into the studio system - it needed guys like Mann to pry open the studio ceiling and let a little light and realism in, even if he didn't pursue it any more than he did a perfect image, he just had great instincts. Speaking of which, the supporting cast includes King Donovan, Harry Antrim, Whit Bissell, Jean Hagen, Charles McGraw, Edmon Ryan, James Craig, and Paul Harvey (that's Richard Basehart, uncredited, as a Bank Teller, having been demoted from President of the Cult of the Supreme Being since *Black Book* – *it's fun to think of he and Mann getting along after a few movies, like Steven Soderbergh and George Clooney or Matt Damon*). This New York is hot as hell, with kids selling you caskets, a glass of beer looking like manna from heaven, and bad things coming around every corner for every two-bit dreamer who thought he'd buy his wife a nice new fur coat.

Winchester '73 – 1950

"An Indian would sell his soul to own one..."
Hardly a bright beginning to this quite dark
western, Mann's first. Jimmy Stewart's
natural itchy Americana is starting to grow
strange and tired, like he woke up from his
filibuster and the country hadn't changed at
all. There's nobody honest and virtuous in
Dodge City which Stewart's canvassing
(with a shooting contest as sting) looking
for an outlaw named Dutch Henry Brown
(Stephen McNally). Marshall Wyatt Earp
(Will Geer) and his brother Virgil (Guy
Wilkerson) take his gun and take him to the
saloon. Millard Mitchell is Stewart's second,
and between him and Earp, they just about
manage from keeping he and McNally from
killing each other with imaginary six
shooters in the bar. They both reach for
them like phantom limbs. "Money won't buy
it, and it'd be wrong to sell it." He's talking
about the rifle of the title, the prize in a
shootin' match, but he means the soul, too.
Stewart and McNally talk to each other like
jilted lovers; this dynamic, too, seems a
sequel to another classic, Howard Hawks'
Red River if Montgomery Clift and John

Ireland's affair had continued, then ended badly. Stewart would later *play* Wyatt Earp in John Ford's *Cheyenne Autumn.*

"All I need is a beaver hat and I'll be dressed for Easter." The film's structure is a marvelous revision of the oater, with the gun's changing fortunes our anchor more than any of its owners, like the same year's *La Ronde* by Max Ophüls, finally. Perfectly the French film centers on amorous connection between strangers and the American looks at a shooting iron as stand-in for all its country symbolizes. William H. Daniels drinks in the unforgiving light of the desert and its chiaroscuro counterpoints by night, whether in a room with shades to mask a beating or out on the trail as the enemy closes in with murder in his eyes. Daniels had been, in the parlance of *Winchester,* shooting holes in postage stamps like Stewart long before Mann needed a suitable John Alton stand-in. He won an Oscar for *The Naked City* under Jules Dassin's direction, who like Alton and Mann, had been inventing noir's new language at the end of the 40s. He shot a passel of classics for Lubitsch, Stroheim, Cukor, Mamoulian, some minor Wellman, and Clarence Brown's gorgeous *Flesh and the Devil* with Greta Garbo. He (and Mann) is all about atmosphere, as if he were still shooting silent films. He hangs out in the gorgeous environs, every watering hole and desert trading post, and just let tensions simmer in the noon day sun.

"You're beginning to like it..." The gun passes between/before John McIntire's shiftless trader, a grizzled sergeant played by the ever-reliable Jay C. Flippen and his fresh-faced corporal Tony Curtis, good time gal Shelley Winters, angry brave Rock Hudson (Douglas Sirk likes what he sees), Charles Drake's hapless, lying entrepreneur and Dan Duryea's sadistic outlaw. It's both a pleasure and trouble to spend time with each of them, hatred and mistrust and murder behind them, as if bad vibes wore the suits of men. Mann's pursuit of a more relaxed pace (like a snake who knows its prey can't escape) and Stewart, trying to prove he was more than Capra's earnest dreamer, is perfect as a hitch-stepped, dust coated grudge hunter. He wants satisfaction *bad*. When he erupts into violence, you'd almost convinced yourself he wasn't like that, that the man who instinctively grabbed a gun was responding to conditioning, not the direction of his twisted heart. Stewart would continue to let self-loathing and fury and persecution seep into his characters for Mann as the 50s wore on, allowing himself, he who stood in for veterans on the home front, to become a lacerating object, a cancer in the saddle. Hitchcock would take even more advantage of him, turning him into a pervert P.I. and a coercive husband drugging his wife. Even with all these cutthroats around you don't exactly feel safer around him. Evidently this was also the first time an actor received points in exchange for a lower salary.

"You think they'd let a man keeps his hair..." Mann's methodology is deliberately anti-Fordian, with handheld chaos and menacing landscapes suggesting not the beauty and promise of a land but its treachery and deceit. Its haunting and tough, which Ford so rarely chased as a matter of course, but then Mann was always much more eager to mine for frailty. His Wyatt Earp isn't nearly so agreeably stoic as Ford's. The figure Mann cut by now was like Stewart's, heading from place to place, story to story, just doing his best, purpose drilling down wherever he landed. For the first time he wasn't chasing breakneck plot, he was just inhaling behavior, like the romantic look of relief on Stewart's face when he wakes and realizes he's alive and Winters and Mitchell are, too, or Flippen and Winters' brief, abstract flirtation when she escapes death. The Mann landscapes come to seem conjured to enact biblical violence. Nobody can win out here, with guns above and below, and the angry sun judging all of them.

The Furies – 1950

Being out west seemed to calm Mann down *juuuuust* a hair. Or anyway he let conversations transpire across static shots and uses shot-reverse-shot (well that's not fair...maybe shot-boomerang-shot is more the effect) to let the dialogue flow as wide and far as the cattle lands stalked by his heroes. It's a little funny (though of course no surprise) that his noirs were like tours of greasy, grinding machines, cramped and tense and packed tight with treachery. Any minute a spring could snap and the whole thing will fall apart, trapping limbs and fingers and hair in every gear. The westerns are stage plays about frailty and bonds that seem too tight to cut. "I'd bed down with a rattlesnake first," says Walter Huston about disappointing his daughter Barbara Stanwyck. Like Tennessee Williams' Electra she has taken the soul of her mother. She's friendly with her aging father's rival Gilbert Roland, grazing on his land, but pursues Wendell Corey, both of whom secretly wish her father dead. It's the kind of thing that was and would once more make for epics like *Giant, The Big Country,* and *The Leopard,* but Mann's so plainspoken you forget you're watching a film as big as all that. *A Prairie Home Visconti,* complete with wedding dances and unthinkable violence, real and emotional. Walter Huston and Barbara Stanwyck get into each other's faces so much you forget the screen can capture landscapes and herds of cattle, the world itself. What could possibly be more cinematic than their quasi-incestuous bond?

The Furies, unlike the rest of Mann's westerns, is as concerned with private rooms, fireside dealmaking, the cushy but lively atmosphere of T.C. Jeffords' ranch home dead square in the middle of his tracts of land, nicknamed The Furies. Because no man like this would make a home anywhere but the inferno. Mann prowls around the pair, allowing us to come to conclusions as they do; a quick dolly past Stanwyck as she listens to her father start trying to outsmart her tells us he hasn't, and she's a step ahead. Of course, he still knows quite a bit more than she does, not least is how far he'll go to have what he wants; she'll only learn what she can do in impulsive, seething response. It didn't used to matter when she was a kid, but she isn't anymore. Now they're playing for keeps. Stanwyck would play the Huston part herself in a few years in Sam Fuller's peerless *Forty Guns*. Mann cribs from Welles' *Ambersons* in just the right doses, with the homey brick of the Furies homebase standing in stark contrast to the deep wood and unforgiving shadow of Amberson Manor but the tempestuous domestic dramas are no less biting, the rattlesnake always just out of view. "You stop telling lies about me I'll stop telling the truth about you." A big difference between Welles and Mann is Welles moved the camera to explore the mind but called it the world. Mann stayed still, let the world and its madness come to him, with all haste. Welles's camera bristled. Mann's compositions bristle. *Rattle*, even. Subtle, but expressive difference.

This film springs from one too-close encounter with destiny to the next, pleasantries turning to ice between cuts. Flirtation between Stanwyck and Corey is answered in their next meeting with an attempted drowning, and then...cake. These people are unwell. They are America itself. Sick with lust, dewy with avarice, dying to kill. "Swindled is a *harsh* word..." Stanwyck plays her budding cynicism *beautifully,* Corey his oily luxury, Huston his royalty like a cowhide Henry II. A great sequence has Stanwyck staring down a room full of creditors with her back to the camera, emanating coldness, turning her back on her girlhood. A rare and lovely thing: a western entirely from the perspective of a young woman, whose emotions are the lynchpin of every major decision. She looks to the other older woman around her (Judith Anderson, Beulah Bondi, Blanche Yurka) not as models but cautionary tales, sops from the attention she so craves. She wants to be her father, though perhaps she just wants to kill him and wear his skin. *Reign of Terror* seems almost conventional when placed next to this, despite its marvelously psychotic technique. Stanwyck shoots a hole in her lover and calls it flirting, throws scissors at a woman's face for daring to be human, and to cap it off Huston hangs a man before letting him love his daughter. Huston didn't live to see the film, and it's a marvelous epitaph, as good as his best work (we might as well just say *Dodsworth)*. This one's got everything, it just moves so quick and at such pitch it can feel like it's only found one piece of the ankle to bite down on. The poison runs through the whole body.

Devil's Doorway – 1950

Gerald Peary discovered this movie late in life, but just in time to speak at the 2024 John and Francis Ford Film Festival in Portland, Maine. When the subject of Ford's more progressive westerns came up, Gerry was ready with counterprogramming. Forget *Fort Apache, Devil's Doorway* had the goods. This was a film with a native protagonist who is always right (played, disappointingly, by Robert Taylor, who isn't merely white, but the whitest actor who ever lived; stiff, sun chapped, conservative, desperately ugly; there wasn't a thing going for Taylor) and has to fight off agents of white supremacy. Within minutes of arriving home after fighting for the Union he's being called out by scumbags at the local watering hole. "You can always smell 'em," says Louis Calhern, a racist bromide whites have used against every non-white person in America at some point, which means Mann intended this to speak to a country rediscovering its old hatreds after having put them briefly aside for the sake of the war effort.

The post-war Western was a psychological blank ready to be filled in with the new colors of traumatized men on hard times who fought for a country that didn't have room for them. Indeed the term "psychological western" is unavoidable when reading criticism about Mann. These films were maybe less celebrated en masse by the culture than the noir of the same time for their dead-center gaze at the country's fraying seams, but they were no less loud about their intentions and certainly no less seen. Between this, *The Furies,* and his upcoming Jimmy Stewart films, Mann was releasing some of the most lacerating anti-American movies of all time. Something was *wrong* with this country. Luckily we diagnosed the problem, caught it just in time and... let it rot us from the inside out.

John Alton shoots the film in claustrophobic close-ups, the expanses of the west *just* out of frame, their promise of a new beginning, too. It's over before it starts for Taylor's dreams. He should have known better than to fight for a country only too happy to kill him during and after the war. Taylor all but kidnaps the white doctor in town to tend to his dying father, anticipating Don Siegel's Elvis movie *Flaming Star,* and then Calhern takes his family land and prevents him from even being able to buy a drink in his hometown saloon (a plot point in the following year's Val Lewton produced *Apache Drums,* directed by Hugo Fregonese). Not even the intervention of a moral white lawyer (Paula Raymond) is enough to fix it. It never is. Neither allies nor representation can fix a system this purposeful. And she tellingly fails Taylor's character's own anti-HUAC test. She sides with the whites over land rights in her heart, even if she fights for Taylor legally. Master's tools, master's house. Violence alone seems the medicine for this bunch of cowards. "Civilization's a great thing..." moans reluctant sheriff Edgar Buchanan. The law takes his footing as a friend out from under him. How can you call a man a friend when your job asks you to take his freedom?

Storm clouds fall, thunder crashes, and sweaty faces jut into frame like gargoyles, as abrasive and judgmental as any in Fellini. This one's as rough and mean and dark as any of Mann and Alton's films noir, though it might be even more bleak. Mann was taking aim at our foundational myth, and he was among the first white male directors to admit it was horseshit. This was what gave us all this grazing space, all that "elbow room" in the parlance of *Schoolhouse Rock*. Theft and misery and picking fights with Native American Medal of Honor recipients, anticipating Clint Eastwood's *Flags of our Fathers*. It also says that the right political channels don't help the downtrodden when push comes to shove because no one wants the country to work that way anyhow, not anyone who "matters."

With someone other than Taylor in the lead this film would probably be held aloft as one of the most important westerns ever made, ditto Budd Boetticher's *Seminole,* which trades *Devil's Doorway's* sweltering monochrome for gorgeously garish color, and to a lesser extent Sirk's *Taza, Son of Cochise, b*oth of which have to make do with an unproven Rock Hudson for star power. A bar fight with a racist (who shoots at Taylor but can't make him flinch) is both expertly edited and shot (townsfolk's faces hiding in all corners, watching, mute and demonic) and the last victory Taylor will know. Street justice. Take it or accept destruction. They'll kill you and they get to tell people why they did it. What do you do? When your hand goes for a gun, will you let it? These are ugly questions, but they're not unfair. Not in this country. Gerry was right...Ford never quite came out and said it like this.

The Tall Target – 1951

"Mr. Lincoln's a tall target, there'll be another day," is a perfect bit of tossed off poetry, like Harry Lime's "cuckoo clock" parable in *The Third Man.* Once more linking Mann to Orson Welles, *The Tall Target* builds a film around an absence. No Lincoln, no law, no justice, etc. No Harry Lime, no one held accountable for the moral dereliction and dead kids in Vienna. They're both films about detectives in long coats divining and possibly protecting the direction of a country. They're beautifully optimistic works because they imagine such a thing is possible and that little men can do just this. But more than relishing in ideals protected by these actions, the films are all momentum, which is what counts.

Mann may have actually idolized Lincoln privately (and casting Adolphe Menjou as his traitorous would-be assassin seems to speak to a rejection of the popular politics of the 1950s) but it's not remotely a problem that the film could well be just another assignment, like *He Walks By Night*. It's a perfect potboiler and personal in gesture and construction. Had I been given a Sight and Sound ballot in 2022 I'd have had a hard time talking myself out of including it, even if *Black Book* is the more impressive work on its face.

It's 1861 and Dick Powell has infiltrated a gang of hardliners, knowing they plan to kill Lincoln at his inauguration. He can't make anyone believe him and he resigns in disgrace and heads to the train station to get down south and stop the plot in person. An associate is meant to give him his ticket on the train but when Powell arrives the man is dead and there's someone else aboard (Leif Erickson, perfectly oily) claiming to *be* Powell. So he's got no proof he's who he says he is, no back-up arriving, and a train full of partisans who could be fatally against his cause. Right away three unstoppable outfits for a work to wear:

political conspiracy, period noir, and a train movie. And all directed by Mann in under 80 minutes. There is no more perfect vehicle of the cinema than the train. The camera is itself its closest analog, a device that eats and slows time and presents otherwise impossible things, that collects strangers for a voyage through darkness. When you exit the cinema you're in a different place than when you entered. *This* is why *The Tall Target* may indeed be a better movie than *Black Book*. Its series of nocturnal navigations and erotic interruptions, of Powell weaving in and out of people's private spaces and their lives along with them for a few tense moments, drag you into womb spaces, quiet but for the rattle of the rails, spaces we'd never otherwise know. Mann's low angles strand Powell in the long night as he wonders and demonstrates how many and how few places there are to hide on a train. The locomotive is his proving ground and his playground, no person a real part of his story until they wake up or catch him invading their cabin. Cinematographer Paul C. Vogel films every pocket of steam and overhead light with the nerves of a paranoiac and the specificity of Caravaggio (this is likely his best work, though Ford's *The Wings of Eagles,* and Robert Montgomery's first-person thriller *Lady in the Lake* are exquisite runners-up). Death or the theft of your being in the very next car.

The film's arrested time is some kind of magic trick. In 80 minutes we truly feel every second of the long night's ride from Boston to Baltimore, a train trip I've made many times. A specialty of cinema specifically is making us feel strapped to characters undergoing transformative hours of their lives. Powell's tribulations are never ending and range from great comfort to brawling beneath the train's wheels. This is the action hero's lot, of course, but there's such a beautifully ordered flow to it. He knows he's just going to be rocked around until well after dawn. His body is on the line for his country, but he never makes more than passing mention of the things that depend on his success. Jumping cars and hiding in bunks, the perimeters of his mission become abstract until he's confronted with people in relative comfort. He's keenly aware of the absurdity of his outward appearance because life goes by for everyone else with the calming certainty of the sights and sounds that pass by their window. Out there is just the world, until it penetrates the stillness of an overnight train ride. Then, suddenly, it's all very real. As it always has been for millions. The promise of the train: what can you do on a moving train cut off from any country or allegiance or purpose? That's why the perversion of its promised isolation is so perfect. Nothing is *meant* to happen between stations. You don't exist in your society on a train. You belong to no nation, levitating off the ground until you arrive. This is also true in a movie theater...unless someone makes a film where people are trying to kill Abraham Lincoln. You discover what country you want to live in then. When Menjou has to leave a backwards message on a window in the snowy morning chill and take it on faith his similarly backwards work will be carried out, you hold your breath (flashes of Janet Leigh's car in the swamp in *Psycho*). The power of an image and an idea. Could it all really hinge on something so small?

The cast of auxiliary characters are pungent with details. All Powell has to do is mention Lincoln in a crowded car and he gets a free group diagnosis. Paula Raymond is a spoiled heiress, Marshall Thompson her strident soldier brother, and Ruby Dee is their slave; Mann and writers Daniel Mainwaring, Art Cohn, and George Worthing Yates make your hair stand on end watching Raymond dance around the subject of Ruby Dee's place in her life. She takes umbrage at the idea that her people beat their slaves and indeed wishes to let it be known that she too suffered at the hands of Dee's white 'betters', all but inventing the worst and most selfish millennial posture ("hearing the key in the door was my own "antebellum south" for almost 20 years"). Would you believe she ends the film slapping Dee with the butt of a gun while calling her sister? Florence Bates is a nosy dowager who wants to know all about Dee's experiences being beaten by her masters. "We don't have slaves in Boston..." she coos, unaware what a bitter laugh that line would get today. Mainwaring was a reliable purveyor of left-leaning potboilers, from Siegel's *Invasion of the Body Snatchers* and Phil Karlson's *The Phenix City Story.* Here's me on Mainwaring in an *Invasion of the Body Snatchers* piece I wrote around the same time as I wrote this: "you don't write the excoriating *Phenix City Story* at a time when screenwriters are being blacklisted left and right *and* finally allow yourself to be credited under your own name (instead of his long-in-use pseudonym Geoffrey Homes) without knowing *precisely* what you're doing. *Phenix City* is as much a companion piece to *Body Snatchers* as *Riot in Cell Block 11.* Both *Riot* and *Body Snatchers* are about dehumanization in enclosed environments desperate for word to reach the outside world) and *Phenix's City's* tale of a city falling under the thumb of a powerful racket killing everyone who threatens to undermine their operation is only a genre away. Even the idea of the aliens coming in pods brings to mind the quelling of farm and migrant laborers strikes as seen in John Ford's *The Grapes of Wrath.* The final hiding place McCarthy and Wynter attempt is a mine, still a synecdoche for unions attempting to keep their members alive, as seen in another Ford film *How Green Was My Valley.* Siegel and Mainwaring would once more stick up for the little guy by having Mickey Rooney's Baby Face Nelson refuse to bump off a union organizer in their hardboiled biopic of the psychotic gangster." George Worthing Yates was a Brooklyn boy who wrote quite boyish movies from 1938's *The Lone Ranger* to about a dozen monster movies (an impressive collection that features *Them!, It Came From Beneath The Sea, Attack of the Puppet People*). Art Cohn would likely have gotten more done than the dozen movies he wrote (including Rossellini's *Stromboli!*) if he hadn't followed Mike Todd aboard The Lucky Liz, the super producer's private jet, that day in 1958. Turns out she wasn't that lucky.

And then there's Menjou, whose big reason for killing the president is cotton futures. He's such a soft, paternalistic figure with his bedside bourbon and his reedy nattering. He's exactly the sort of person who gets away with ruining millions of lives because he won't stand for living in less than total comfort. It's wild to hear Thompson explain his rationale for killing Lincoln to Dee's face, but it's also completely accurate. Fascists do it all the time. They're doing it right now while the bodies of children are being pulled from rubble that used to be the Gaza Strip. There's comfort in a film so handsomely clad in a costume drama's trappings, so lithe and alive with the rough pleasures of espionage, but it also doesn't shirk its responsibilities as something more than entertainment. To occupy the public's time is one thing. To reach them another. A film can be a rollercoaster and a poem at once. Mann knew it, and in this, his finest film, he achieves the perfect synthesis of real and false, action and silence, the political and the personal.

Bend of the River – 1952

Anthony Mann was flown into Rome to work on some background sequences on the spectacularly dull *Quo Vadis,* about the burning of Rome (spoiler alert: Nero fiddles). Mervyn LeRoy made the film, Mann just did a little second unit, and so much the better because the idea of watching it twice didn't much appeal to me. Robert Taylor as a centurion. No, indeed. Once was enough. But it must have lit a fire under Mann to start the third phase of his career. He'd emerge in color on big sets and bigger landscapes, and they'd continue to write his thesis on the treachery of the human spirit. *Bend of the River* was his second western with Jimmy Stewart but the first where they seem fully in sync, wherein Stewart fought against the "Aw Shucks!" stock type he fit so well working for Capra and Cukor. His Mann heroes would be complicated men with ugly things on their minds, and the films would lay out miles of craggy, desolate country on which their passions would be painted, and the dead dirt country roads and hard mountainous terrain would reflect back at these men the lack in their spirits.

This one takes a few hard turns right from the jump. Stewart's name is Glyn McLyntock, leading a wagon train, amiably flirting with some of its women, and then he turns the wrong corner and there in close-up is Arthur Kennedy's neck in a noose. Stewart scares off the party and then realizes he and Kennedy know a little of each other, and it's not all good. Is he gonna regret taking him down off the cross, so to speak? Kennedy hasn't been in camp five minutes before they're hearing "birds", really a war party staking out the train as it beds down for the night. The suddenness of the arrow that hits Julie Adams in the shoulder shocks us. Mann treats the cuts like violence itself, not allowing the wider spaces to offer any kind of reprieve from bloodshed and combat, real and psychological. The teeming communities would seem the kind of place these men could start over ("I'm running away from a man named Glyn Mclyntock." says Stewart, afraid of who he was and even more afraid he might still be that man).

They land in Portland Oregon, rendered as a lovely riverboat dock town, a marvel of production design, the kind Mann would have seen at Cinecitta working on *Quo Vadis,* and it too has its fair share of shady characters (oh... Stepin Fetchit's here, giving one of his more nuanced performances, for whatever that's worth...). Rock Hudson's a gambler with an itchy trigger finger. He kills Frank Ferguson over a hand of poker ten minutes after Lori Nelson sees him and is instantly smitten. Everybody's a killer and if they're not they oughta be real soon or they won't see the end credits. There's a montage of tree clearing as Stewart and his wagon train leave Portland city center for the surrounding countryside; master the land or become part of the landscape. Jay C. Flippen has to leave daughter Adams in Portland to recuperate and when he returns to get her a gold rush has made the place even more busy and cutthroat. Howard Petrie has come in and gouged prices to deal with the influx of new blood in town and Kennedy's working for him and dating Adams. Neither sits well with Stewart and Flippen. The mobster capitalism that was Mann's pet subject in the late 40s has followed him like his own shadow out into the west. An argument with Petrie becomes a shooting match in no time at all, with Kennedy and Hudson stepping into the breach with Stewart on pure instinct. Exciting, all the more so because we know they can't put their differences aside forever.

"Seemed like a real nice fella." "He was... 'til he found gold." As the party retreats into the hills with supplies stolen from the greedy Portland mogul the members of the small party turn on each other. Stewart gets beaten up good and Kennedy sides with the duplicitous hired help when he hears there's money in it. Kennedy makes a fatal mistake and lets Stewart live, because of course he does. Now every time something goes wrong, every shadow out of place, Kennedy imagines Stewart is out there trying to kill him and paranoia never makes for effective leadership. The party starts to thin, along with the collective nerve of the hired guns. Kennedy's disintegration becomes the film's main event, a flamboyant display of blown composure, which unfortunately means we lose Stewart for much of the final act, a miscalculation which could account for the bad reviews this received. The film almost makes Stewart the kind of anti-hero he'd play to the hilt in the next few Mann westerns, but the reveal of his hanging rope scarred neck is too little too late. Still, it's quite a picture. It just never becomes a pantheon classic.

The Naked Spur – 1953

Bend of the River has virtues but was about the most conventional film Anthony Mann had made in six years, and it in no way hinted at the coiled formalist of *Raw Deal* or the ingenious provocateur of *Black Book.* Mann talked about landscapes defining performances and characters and now that he was out in them, business as usual wouldn't do. The lush California and Colorado scenery seems to mock anti-hero Jimmy Stewart, finally shedding the skin of the likable everyman and allowing himself to broil with the kind of anger that was beginning to define the post-war male. In Westerns the civil war was always in the rearview mirror, and our heroes are now innocent of purpose and rules. Stewart is chasing Robert Ryan with the help of the desperately untrustworthy Ralph Meeker (just dishonorably discharged from the cavalry and still wearing the striped pants of the uniform, on the run from a tribe of Blackfeet out for vengeance after he dishonored the chief's daughter) and the just plain desperate Millard Mitchell, both of whom want the money on Ryan's head more than they care about Stewart's non-existent authority. Watching all the fireworks is Ryan's girl Janet Leigh, who, by way of introduction, bites Meeker's gun hand. It's a free-for-all of conflicting egos, a tangle of rats caught by the tail who have discovered the freedom the West promises means there's no framework for civilization. Or as Meeker says when he gets the drop on Ryan. "That's life..."

Stewart's way out on a limb here, lying and compromising whatever morals he had left in order to make sure Ryan hangs for murder. Ryan lays it all out for Leigh - if he's gonna cheat the hangman he needs to stall Stewart as much as possible, and that means killing her favourite horse first of all and a lot worse besides. Leigh is styled as a near feral adolescent with her short hair, filthy second hand clothes, and her love for the man who killed her father in a bank job in Abilene. Nobody here remembers the hand of progress. Meeker tries to have his way with her almost immediately after they shoot her horse and spends the whole next act like a circling vulture, gawking and cackling over her while he plans to kill her man. Ryan never lets it slip that he's licked, laughing and joking as they march him to his death. Soon the boys start doing the math about the 50,000 dollar reward on Ryan's head. Lots of ways tor a man to die in the mountains... be a shame if that three-way split turned two-way...or one...

There's an attack by the Blackfeet at the start of act 2 in which Stewart tries to throw Meeker to them to save himself and keep Ryan intact for hanging, and there's no music. It's a quick, violent little skirmish and when it's over the smell of gunpowder and death hangs in the air. No victory took place here, and no heroes walk away from it. Stewart's fever dreams speak of broken promises and afterwards he starts nursing his own humanity back to health. Leigh starts to warm to him, which is kind of a copout; she knew Ryan was a psycho all these weeks before Stewart showed up, uncertain why Stewart's folksiness seems like the ideal alternative if they had the chemistry they appeared to early on, but hey, the human heart is wild. "That's something else, I'm talking to you now," says Stewart, dead serious when she reminds him he plans to kill Ryan, which does make up for the screenwriting contrivance required to get to such a smoldering delivery. And then mere minutes later he challenges Ryan to a quickdraw contest in a cave. The wide world wasn't fit for them. Heavy breathing murderers goading each other in darkness. Mann hadn't quite looked this hard at us before. The comforting fantastical long gone.

Thunder Bay – 1953

We're always dimly aware that the big directors from the 20s through the 60s, the studio heyday in America, were prone to necessary detours. Producers had movies they wanted made, the public suddenly took an interest in an issue or an actor, and someone's got to stand behind the camera and call "action!" in every such case. It must have been exciting when a director and actor found each other in the midst of such a climate, and indeed Jimmy Stewart and Anthony Mann found each other *hard*. Like Steven Soderbergh and Channing Tatum, or Martin Scorsese and Leonardo DiCaprio, they wanted in on each other's schemes halfway through peculiar careers and made some fine, tough work together. Mann and Stewart made five westerns together and three other films, *Thunder Bay*

160

being the first of the latter. It was a big to-do at the time, planned in 3D but released in 2D, shot 1.37 but stretched to 1.85 for release, and Universal-International's first film with stereophonic sound. They wanted a big-ticket Stewart film, a contemporary spectacle and Mann gave them one, a kind of proto-*Giant* or *Written on the Wind,* but with neither's ambition for mythic anthropology or sexual insanity. This was another Mann/Stewart western in all but setting, and Mann quite understandably expressed his dissatisfaction with it. It's too little and too obvious at almost every turn.

Stewart is an enterprising oilman who has come to intercept the more established Jay C. Flippen and sell him his new design for an offshore rig. The clean lines of the exaggerated color from the blown up and blown out print work like gangbusters in this scene (the reds and greens fade in and out like chameleon skin thanks, I think, to the aborted 3D), with Flippen and Stewart intoxicating each other with capitalist bluster. The old man agrees and soon Stewart and partner Dan Duryea, returning from Mann's *The Great Flamarion* along with Erich von Stroheim's cinematographer

William H. Daniels, are hard at work building a big, gleaming, phallic derrick in order to gut the gulf and defile some daughters along with the landscape while they're at it. Local fishermen Gilbert Roland and Antonio Moreno are happy to have the influx of money at first, until it becomes clear that drilling for oil means disturbing the local shrimping industry. Moreno's daughters Marcia Henderson and Joanne Dru are intrigued and repulsed by Stewart and Duryea, respectively, and everyone will learn a lot before both men leave town, if they can do so before Roland stirs the other fishermen into a murderous frenzy.

For a movie called *Thunder Bay,* it's not Canadian or sensational enough and all too linear. Injunctions are filed, protests are mounted and abandoned, bar fights and parties feel all too rehearsed. I was reminded of Fregonese's *Blowing Wild* and Nicholas Ray's *Wind Across the Everglades,* but never in a good way. *Blowing Wild* isn't Hugo's best, but at least it gets a fire going under the central trio of Barbara Stanwyck, Anthony Quinn, and Gary Cooper and there's a bunch of murder and mayhem. Stewart's best quality is his simplicity, which is what makes his perversion so compelling in *Vertigo* and his murderous frustration so scary in *The Naked Spur;* where was he hiding it? It's why he's so watchable in the early funny ones, he brims with pet dog eagerness. As a strapping capitalist, wielding dynamite against angry mobs and calling the shots at sea, he's in bad need of a different kind of edge. Maybe Gregory Peck's as Ahab in *Moby Dick*. This is a part for *Wild's* Cooper, or John Wayne, or Clark Gable; someone a little more strapping. Stewart can't lose, it's the 50s, and there's no particular danger he'll get close. At one point he shouts "There's oil out there! And *someone's* got to get it!" inventing Daniel Plainview in *There Will Be Blood*. The movie never gets around to disagreeing with him, which isn't the *whole* problem, but it's emblematic of the rest of them. Minor pleasures: a hurricane-set fist fight and Jay C. Flippen, never a marquee name but the kind of actor real heads trust to get every kind of job done in style, giving a heartbreaking bedside speech, one of those great solos he was only allowed every once in a while.

The Glenn Miller Story – 1954

Anthony Mann said the reason he was enticed to make *The Glenn Miller Story* was that he was interested in the idea of making sound and music visual, a perfect filmmaking-engineering project. "...I wanted to dramatize a sound. And it's the story of finding a new sound... to tell the story of a man who is hunting something new and finally finds it..." Ironically the film was released in mono, though it was recorded in stereo, which does rather undercut the idea of making a movie about music. Glenn Miller was both a nationally admired band leader and a war hero, so there was no way Mann was going to make the kind of movie he did best - this was his first biopic, but sadly not his last. Mann got his start with musicals so this was a return to form but it wasn't exactly a secret he made noirs and westerns about 1000 times better than he made musicals. Not to say he was a slouch or anything but with Jimmy Stewart, himself a war hero, telling the story of another war hero, the odds this could have the same sacrilegious energy of his best work were slim but he snuck in some good filmmaking.

A dead broke horn player named Glenn Miller (Stewart) keeps getting booted from clubs and auditions until one day he gives a stack of arrangements, freshly written, to drummer and bandleader Ben Pollack (playing himself). He gets a gig with his band The Californians and this enables him to reunite with Helen a girl who had long forgotten him (June Allyson). The movie makes it clear that there's very little Glenn Miller can't make happen through sheer force of will. He's got that stick-to-itiveness that we love in our American icons. He's late in picking Helen up, but he won't take 'no' for an answer. When her anger melts and his bluster fades they have *gorgeous* chemistry. "Why can't I ever stay mad at you?" She laughs and he chuckles right back. "I don't know!" He marries her and gets a job in a pit orchestra along with Benny Goodman and Gene Krupa, also playing themselves. Miller and Helen save a little money to put a band together but his dream keeps falling apart, not least because of their inability to have children.

Mann's form is comparatively staid for a lot of the runtime, shooting in handsome wides and mediums and not cutting unless he has to, but not reinventing the wheel either. Now there's method to the lack of madness, because when music becomes a part of the spectacle, the film really comes alive, and well, a jazz song has to have a melody before the artists can solo if you catch my drift. Ben Pollack's first drum kit attack reminds you how exciting it can be to watch a drummer, or more broadly a musician, *cook*. When Miller and Allyson get hitched and jazz musicians crash their wedding night and head to a club and Louis Armstrong is there, Mann starts clumsily flipping color gels in front of the lens to make sure we can see the playing but also make us aware that to be able to play like Krupa and Armstrong is indeed like seeing the world in color for the first time, purple and green. It's a gift and Mann does his best to let live playing (and pretty well synched pre-records) tell the story. The old Mann rears up every so often (dig the funicular going diagonally behind Stewart looking into a shop window, creating for a moment, an angle John Alton would have helped him achieve just a few years

166

earlier). There's real intelligence in pacing and transition, like a shot of Miller's muddy feet after his car gets stuck; this is a working-class band, no different from the dreamers who steal in his noirs. Soon he's in the army, a Captain with a commission, and before long he'll board a plane home and never get off.

Stewart, meanwhile, is the kind of actor who can do the impossible: make a biopic's hoariest cliches feel like genuine inspiration. When he writes "Moonlight Serenade" he and Allyson have to name it as he plinks away gently at it on the piano. You almost believe it happened like this. Stewart sitting in darkness composing a new clarinet melody to the song, touching the piano between pencil notations as the camera slowly backs out is a lovely way to add urgency to the otherwise serene sounds. With a little more time and money, he's able to return to the Busby Berkeley style musical/visual motifs he couldn't when he was in the business of song and dance, like a rotating image of records in a jukebox or those geometrically pleasing images of the band lined up to blow their horns, the frame split in daring scalene shapes. He was attempting to come up with a visual language that went with the bending and sliding of a note on a horn. He even films the band scoring a movie, a re-purposing of the rear projection in *Black Book*. The film may never develop the heart rate required to truly transpose Jazz (even Jazz as bog standard as Miller's) but it's beautiful to watch him inject a rather ordinary film with these flights into the stratosphere. The film can be best summed up in the scene where Miller puts a jazz beat under a march for a general at an air base. Art needn't move at life's pace.

The Far Country – 1954

Universal-International allowed Anthony Mann access to stars and money and splashy technicolor film, but they were less interested in Mann's more uncomfortable political thrillers. While he made *Winchester '73, Bend of the River, Thunder Bay,* and *The Far Country* for Universal, it was MGM that allowed him to make *The Tall Target, The Naked Spur, The Furies,* and *Devil's*

Doorway. *The Far Country* was his last film for UI, and it begins with a bang. Jimmy Stewart rides into town with a herd of cattle, tips his cap at employer Walter Brennan, then turns to two guys on his crew and says "Here are your guns…alright you've been waiting for 500 miles, go ahead and use 'em." They don't take the bait. "I'll live to see you hang…" spits one of them and they ride off. Now *that's* not a bad way to start a picture. The refusal to implicate either party and us in the process speaks to the limitation of Universal's vision of the human spirit during this early 50s jag, so does the spritely patchwork score (music by Henry Mancini, Hans Salter, Frank Skinner and Herman Stein gets carelessly repurposed throughout). This isn't a hard look at humanity. It's sort of a horseback caper until it's arbitrarily a little more serious.

Stewart's men report him for murder for unseen doings during his latest cattle drive. He and Brennan board a boat for Dawson City up in the Klondike (a place Bill Morrison fans know well as the spot where exhibition film reels used to dead-end after their distribution runs) and the police board to try to take him into custody. Stewart outmaneuvers them and then Ruth Roman invites him into her bed to act as her alibi, prefiguring Eva Marie Saint's rescue of Cary Grant aboard the train to Chicago in *North By Northwest.* So now two mysteries: what does Roman want from Stewart and what did Stewart do out there on the trail? This will all become clear after they deposit their cattle and settle in Skagway, Alaska (good name), run by iron fisted Judge Gannon (John McIntire). He also gets involved with the local French doctor (Eugene Borden) and his daughter (Corinne Calvet, so fetching in Ford's *When Willie Comes Marching Home,* so very like a live action Pippi Longstocking here…) and a drunken prospector played by Jay C. Flippen. Appealingly the Judge holds his trials at the local gambling hall while Roman, in puffy sleeves and bare shoulders, watches from behind the bar. A lot more justice might get served if there was whiskey in court. Skagway isn't quite a Fordian utopia or a Hawksian dystopia (Mann, for all his gifts, couldn't get so firm a grip on setting; his atmosphere was ephemeral and traveled, and so no one place gets to grow much in our estimation, and no space becomes his signature) but it's fun to spend time here.

McIntire takes Stewart's cattle as punishment for the murder and they part as enemies, but Roman hires Stewart and Brennan right back to take the herd to Dawson anyway. Gannon's not gonna like that… Some folks suspect that Gannon was based on Soapy Smith, the real degenerate con artist mayor of Skagway during the Gold Rush, who met a similar fate. The film is enhanced by the towering Alberta mountains in the back of every shot. Mann, like Peter Jackson after him, luxuriates in the natural scenery as the men travel toward their destiny. The landscape dwarfs their earthly concerns, and makes absurd every drawn gun and tossed insult, which is good because the film needs a little more friction than the script is willing to provide. Roman V. Calvet is a non-starter, only the former has any sex appeal, and Stewart romancing young women is always creepy and paternalistic. He was many things but 'erotic' wasn't one of them. Jay C. Flippen and Walter Brennan are naturally great as his sidekicks, but they don't *do* anything. Stewart's misanthropy isn't quite as compelling here (Roman and her crew are trapped in an avalanche, and he doesn't want to help them until Calvet forces his hand) as it is in *Bend of the River or The Naked Spur* because it's not his character that's on trial. Here he just looks craven and business-minded but he's still the hero and the film doesn't forget that so readily. Stewart's eagerness to let Roman freeze to death makes their flirtation afterwards seem a little more disconcerting than it is wrong in the fun, adult way. This is a shame because Roman positively seethes in this one, a Mannish woman worthy of Stanwyck in *The Furies*. It'd be nice to think Stewart was her equal, but it's not that kind of film. It has heroes. The best Mann films have to squint to find those.

The film's micro drawbacks become part of a macro scheme in the final act. As Skagway and Dawson never develop enough personality, we only get to know their people a few at a time. A little more ambition could have helped the final act. Dave Kehr compared it to Ford in its aspiration to show the changing of a sociopolitical tide, though it's reflected through a very limited perspective, namely

Stewart's. Indeed, the best scene in the film has Stewart looking at the hand he intends to commit a murder with as if it were the only part of him that takes lives, some other separate piece; it's all one body, a lesson Stewart learns as he finally allows himself to become part of a community. You can't shoot without an arm and a community is nothing without people. So he must finally take a side that isn't his own, though by definition it must also be that. McIntire's eccentricity helps keep him aloft as a worthy boogeyman until the final reel. The lessons learned in *The Naked Spur* expand to impact a town's worth of people. But solidarity comes at a price. Your conscience always does.

Strategic Air Command – 1955

In *The Glenn Miller Story* a military brass band has to compete with an air raid siren and the sound of a crashing German plane, which acts almost as an attention-stealing solo from the jazz (like the sound of a subway train stealing attention from the

Clash song "Up In Heaven (Not Only Here)"
maybe the song I've gotten the most
mileage out of as an arts critic). With
Strategic Air Command, Mann was giving
the airplanes and pilots their own concerto.
Jimmy Stewart really flew planes during the
second world war and starred in a PSA for
Air Force pilots directed by John Huston
(mostly it's stock footage and a single
camera set-up on Stewart hanging out of a
plane and talking directly and delicately to
camera about syphilis). Part of what made
Stewart so perfect for Hitchcock and Mann
was he seemed so uncertain about how
truly grotesque his desire and anger would
read on film. When a guy this affable
suddenly snaps and shows you what's
behind his patriotic good old boy mask,
something really ugly and creepy sneaks
out. Thank God Stewart was so
unselfconscious a man (though of course,
ironically, he was a really self-conscious
performer, seemingly constantly trying to
make his audience comfortable with the
fact that they're sitting in a movie with him,
watching him get picked up by that big
VistaVision camera) because if he knew
what people could get out of him he might
have guarded himself against it.

Hammering home the Jimmy Stewart Thing™ *Strategic Air Command* opens at a baseball game. Returning from the last passel of Mann/Stewart films are June Allyson, Jay C. Flippen, Alex Nicol, Harry Morgan, James Bell, James Millican and Don C. Harvey (the last two, like co-star Frank Lovejoy, were both dead not long after this was in the can). Stewart plays a prolific flier during the second world war and the Air Force want him back to do some Cold War deterrent action. Lovejoy plays the general who drafts Stewart back into active duty after so many years away from the stick. He's modeled after Curtis "Bombs Away" LeMay, one of those stars and bars psychos who was always a whiskey sour away from starting World War 3 (Malcolm Gladwell wrote a jaw-dropping book celebrating him and other ultraviolent 'heroes' that's completely absent a psychological dimension, which is just how Gladwell lives), while Stewart's was ostensibly based on Clifford Schoeffler, but also resembles Teddy Williams - although this is all roughly what Stewart's own biography looked like if you swap out relief on the Arizona Cardinals for making westerns. He was a colonel when he retired

(Reagan made him a Major General in between setting fire to corners of the map of Latin America and the Middle East) and he even flew a mission during the Vietnam War! Guess he was just feeling patriotic, as Brendan James says of torture advocate Jonathan Alter.

If you hadn't pieced it together by now this is one dull fucking movie. It's Mann so it never fully loses momentum but there's just so much cinematic intrigue that can be gained from demonstrations of flight training and airplane engineering. Stewart cared too much to let anything you might call "cinematic" come between him and the mission of the piece whereas a coward like John Wayne didn't mind making the same kind of movie (*The Wings of Eagles*) a broad comedy and a high romantic tragedy in between actual aviation. From the sound of it, Mann did it because he and Stewart got along so well but he also understood that to make it, they needed the full cooperation of the Air Force, and to get that, in the 1950s, you were not to make light of the subject or the uniform. Mann said the characters were (sic) "paper mache" and so concentrated on filming the huge bombers being flown (hilariously they never saw combat and one of them was decommissioned like six months later because it kept breaking down). I suppose there's a kind of...I don't know exactly, broad kitsch avant-garde pleasure to be found in the Thomas Tutwiler aerial photography and the moodier William H. Daniels photography on the ground all while composer Victor Young's great syrupy midcentury symphony is slathered on (note to self: re-edit this movie). But this is no sane person's definition of great cinema. Naturally it was a huge box office success and recruitment numbers spiked. God bless America.

The Man From Laramie – 1955

Anthony Mann worked hard to pull himself out of the quickie B movie ghetto, creating some of the great works of art of the 40s and 50s out of grit, determination, and a little elbow grease. The budgets were small, the scripts sometimes unpolished, but his touch was always felt. With *The*

Man from Laramie Columbia put the final nail in the coffin of Mann's career as a slick small timer getting away with murder thanks to great surfeits of style. He was finally shooting in bigger than life Cinemascope with one of the biggest stars in America (though of course this was his and Stewart's eighth and final collaboration). Though it'd be tempting to say he never looked back, that it was all epics from here on out, the truth is more interesting. Before making the enormously budgeted and just plain enormous *Fall of the Roman Empire* and *El Cid* (and *Spartacus,* though he walked off that one after just a few weeks after setting Kubrick a bear trap of sluggish mise en scène to step in), he made *Men in War,* his darkest film, just a few years later, once more showing the strain and beautiful scars of a low budget. Just when it seemed Mann was fully gentrified, he zagged when others would zig. This, after all, was a film itself about rebelling against one's nature, causing trouble and yanking off band aids in search of justice. "The justice of a rifle", as Aline MacMahon's Kate Canaday says to Stewart after she saves him from a lynching, but someone somewhere would pay for having twisted the country so crooked.

"Hate's unbecoming in a man like you. In some men it *shows*..." is the warning Stewart gets when he steps off a treacherous trail with supplies from Laramie. He isn't here to deliver goods. He's looking for the man who sold repeating rifles to some Apache, the same rifles that ended his little brother's life. When he gets into Coronado, he finds a lot of suspicious minds and plenty of violent hands. Alex Nicol shoots his mules and burns his wagons, Arthur Kennedy runs interference for him, and just when Stewart gets the better of both of them, father Donald Crisp intervenes on their behalf... backed by a dozen guns. This sadistic clan runs this part of the world, including the Apache territory just out of town. Stewart will have justice, one way or the other. And he might have Cathy O'Donnell, too, if Kennedy won't make good on his promise to take her out of Coronado and away from Crisp and Nicol, father and brother. And just what's bleary old Wallace Ford's stake in all this?

Mann wasn't the first director allowed to shoot a Western in Cinemascope, but only a matter of months stopped him. Delmer Daves, Otto Preminger, William Wellman, Henry Hathaway, and Edward Dmytryk got there by a nose and André De Toth was a few minutes behind. Robin Wood called 1958's *Man of the West,* Mann's last western of the 50s, the best Cinemascope picture of that decade, and you can sense Mann still working out how best to make use of all 2.35 of those screen inches. Sometimes it's a matter of putting a horse between actors in conversation or filling the background with a hundred head of cattle. Mann being so attuned to a much tighter frame meant he knew about close-ups and propulsive drama; ways to keep the audience from wondering about things like comparative budgets, and he was one of the best storytellers of his age, sometimes precisely because he'd find visual shortcuts to problems of scale that were so breathtakingly audacious all you could do is surrender or applaud. Out in the open there was nowhere to hide and plenty to hide from. *The Man from Laramie* was the summation of his and Stewart's western revisionism, in which Stewart's anger is wound like a watch whose gears are ready to snap.

The Man from Laramie nicely bridges the gap between your average oater (The Ranown westerns, Mann's own *Naked Spur*) and the epic horse operas (*Giant, Cheyenne Autumn, The Alamo*) that would briefly take over before the genre imploded (like Mann's own *Cimarron,* a bloated mediocrity). As in *The Far Country,* Stewart's own conscious and pride come to stand in for the backbone of a community. If he can't buckle Crisp's stranglehold on Coronado it'll continue to choke on its own fumes, especially if violent and crazy Nicol takes over instead of Kennedy when comes the time for succession. Crisp is going blind, a neat metaphor for the limits of his vision as a baron. Stewart came for one answer but finds a whole passel of them to match the enormity of the frame capturing the great lands Crisp owns. A country that rejects and compartmentalizes the influence of one parent over another will starve for want of the other perspective. As in *The Furies,* a patriarch's grip over his child's will is his undoing, and Aline MacMahon's presence on the other side of the territory, the angel on Stewart's shoulder, is a reminder of the lack of love that's warped the Waggoman family (Fuller's *Forty Guns* was the gender inverse, with *The Furies'* Barbara Stanwyck as the ironfisted matriarch of her own patch of land).

Mann manages a handful of exquisite compositions in between his more functional grammar, but the truth is that the cinemascope frame is needed to provide technical tension. The film's greatest assets are the things that happen when the frame no longer seems so wide, the land so big, the possibilities of the west so vast. After overhearing his father call Kennedy "son," Nicol takes his anger out on Stewart. He and a posse ride up on him and Nicol shoots a hole in his gun hand as Stewart hisses and spits and kicks like a feral animal, his most vulnerable moment in the film. Then they let him go and he walks ten paces before being told to stop. He doesn't turn around. He stands there, two of Nicol's henchmen framing him. The anger packed into that frame is almost as impressive as the composition itself. The film has been compared to *King Lear*, the play Mann wanted most desperately to adapt, and certainly the way the characters withhold information from each other is Shakespearian, but the work it calls to mind for me is *Coriolanus.* Certainly it was hard not to hear this exchange as the movie was heating up for the climax:

-I'll fight with none but thee; for I do hate thee. Worse than a promise-breaker.

-We hate alike.

The Last Frontier – 1955

The Last Frontier has probably the worst optics of any of Mann's westerns, despite the handsome 2.55 aspect ratio and the majestic Mexican locations (Mann would quickly turn back around and film *Serenade* in country). Red Cloud, one of the fiercest and smartest opponents the United States ever tangled with, is made into a simple-minded heel played by Mexican Manuel Dondé, and heroes James Whitmore and Victor Mature keep a native guide with them named *Mungo.* Whitmore is made up to look like Grizzly Adams but Mature looks every bit as old just by virtue of having that face and living that life. They have their furs, collected over a long, harsh season, taken by natives because the local union battalion has run them off their land. They want compensation and to send a message. Mature figures it's the Union what owes him for his stolen goods now that he can't pawn them off on his usual crowd. When they go down to get their just desserts Guy Madison talks them into joining up. So over the course of the picture Mature will have to become a real officer worthy of the Union Blue. The film does ultimately *respect* its native characters but can't help but other them at every turn, even when Mature risks his life to spare a tribe from a massacre.

Two films deep into a brief run of Cinemascope movies and Mann is starting to get the hang of the ratio. A gorgeous crane shot introduces our fort as our three brutes enter from the outside, letting us know they're becoming part of a regiment and, with it, society. He'll return to this shot time and again, knowing what a fine sight

Popocatépetl Volcano is peering out from behind his soldiers and their fort. Dutch tilts in the forest heighten the peril and distance traveled by our characters (interestingly, for a western of this type, the ground surrounding the fort is all hills; no flatland to speak of for most of the runtime). Men are frequently shot and killed at the top of a hill so they can roll down towards the camera. There's a little too much day-for-night but there's great blocking, stretching out platoons and more intimate gatherings across the enormous frame. There's a *gorgeous* shot where half the frame is dedicated to an open door and the other a closed window with Mature standing silhouetted on one side. Real fascinating use of the rectangle.

The film, like most of Mann's westerns, is about little societies standing in for big ones. America was being run by a World War 2 general who just edged out another enormously popular World War 2 general and war in Korea had just been cooked up and abandoned, as Hollywood was turning its biggest stars over to the House Un-American Activities Committee with the implicit backing of its biggest producers.

Mann was right to be asking questions about the tenor of authority. Robert Preston, our black hat heel, has a stain on his ledger (they call him The Butcher of Shiloh) because he's too much of a maniac and gets his guys killed at alarming rates. Who's fit for command? What does it take to lead people? And what kind of future do you make with violence? Mature jokes about finding judges with sympathetic viewpoints after he joins "civilization," the film's great concern. Civilization is what you make work *for* you. And sometimes it's a bunch of ugly bricks walling you off from empathy and beauty. Mature ends up a drunken mess, debasing himself in front of the man he hates before proving himself at the eleventh hour as the movie has no intention of letting anarchy reign supreme.

Time is handled in a very interesting fashion with weeks passing with no indication of the end of a day. The first night Mature gets hammered and meets Anne Bancroft and, seeing as Preston, her husband, is missing and presumed dead, he realizes he's got a good reason to straighten up and fly right. Hey, I'd do just about anything for Anne Bancroft, too, though Mature looks like he was an unsteadily carved children's toy from before fun was invented, so we don't exactly root for him to get the girl. When next we see him, he's made himself known and ingratiated himself with every man in the regiment.

Even more time passes and he goes out to link up with a company heading into Red Cloud's territory and meets the tyrannical Preston for the first time. This was before *The Music Man* steered Preston away from playing western villains and into a much more interesting phase of his career, which lasted decades, though no one much talks about him for some reason. Obviously the earthier Mature laughs more and wants to do all manner of un-biblical things to Bancroft and Preston is bent with notions of duty and honor and position and so can't be anything more than heterosexually polite. Mature throws himself at Bancroft when he confesses to his savagery and she realizes for the first time what kind of a man he is under the starched collar and stiff salutes; the same haggard character who stumbled in from the wilderness at the picture's start. She wants to fight him off and she doesn't want to. In a fairly shocking turn of events Mature leaves Preston to die, comes back to the fort, and everyone who had previously encouraged Mature to think killing him would be a good idea turns on him for doing exactly what they all want to do. He has to go back and get him and apologize for almost killing their commanding officer. If that isn't 'civilization', what is? This snarling little picture is Mann's *Fort Apache,* though it lacks the poetry.

Serenade – 1956

When I worked at Siren Records in Doylestown, Pennsylvania, I had a lot of regulars I loathed. Lawyers with anuran bloat and permanent smiles betraying years of smugly enjoying the penny ante pleasures their race and position had bought them, basement-born cretins so cocked with rage and superiority you worried for people between them and their trucks, for a misplaced step would hit like a heavyweight's cross; gaunt doomsayers with just enough expertise to feel smart and not nearly enough to *be* smart. Everybody had one thing in common: they all wanted a discount on a .99 cent album you'd never listen to twice. We memorized their shuffling gait and amphibious visages and learned to dread their outline as it approached the vestibule. But we had nice regulars, too, most of them squat little fellows who were thrilled to have company who knew about the handful of names they'd held onto in their old age. We were genuinely thrilled to see them, and they were thrilled we talked with them about Jim Nabors. Among this motley crew of peculiar gentlemen was Peter Price, a man who was forever handing in his old records and occasionally special ordering CDs that spoke to a life lived digging through racks for albums beyond the canon. One day Peter and I started talking about movies and he mentioned something that seemed impossible to me: he was once a revered boy soprano and a child actor who had been in movies. Movies *I had seen!* But lo Mr. Price was telling the truth and in fact I'd already seen him as the young Caruso in Richard Thorpe's biopic of the famous singer. Mario Lanza had played the great man as an adult. Lanza died at age 38, ten years younger than Caruso had been when he expired in 1921. Peter lived to be 84 years old, dying in March of 2024, and was always a bright part of my work week. I miss him.

Of course Mr. Price is *not* in Anthony Mann's *Serenade,* Lanza's third-to-last film before his untimely death, and probably the film it is most strange that Anthony Mann made, his other musicals notwithstanding. Even when you do a little math (the Stewart movies, his early jukebox capers, his bloated epics) and suss out what happened, it's just an odd footnote in the middle of a run of movies for men's men. Caruso and Lanza were both heartthrobs, their tenors profundo ringing in the deep and bringing tears to the faces of emotional women and troubled men everywhere on their return. The problem was Lanza himself. He was a heavy drinker and compulsive eater and he never became a great actor. His career was skipping like a stone out of view when Mann was introduced to him, just before it faded completely from sight along with the once-robust gent himself. Mann liked him too much personally to turn him down when it came time to work together, even though in Mann's own words the script was "weak." After all, "how can you tell a story anyway when you're singing arias all the time?" Well...others have managed but Mann was clearly not interested in doing much more than solving the problem of Lanza like a math equation; Roger Corman could have worked wonders with him if only he'd lived a little longer. Mann dutifully opens his 1.85 frame to take in the splendor of Mexican locations and foggy studio sets alike, but he can't quite make the film sing like its star. Mann never made an Elvis film but you do get what it would have looked like after this.

The film was, and you'll have to ratchet on quotation marks the size of the Hollywood sign here, "*Based*" on a novel by James M. Cain. I know what you're thinking because I thought the same thing: No it fucking isn't. And well, the movie, you and I are all correct. Cain's novel is about a male opera singer who fled the spotlight as a migrant worker on a vineyard after he was raped by a promoter and lost his singing voice. A prostitute latches onto him thinking he's gay but he screws her in a church and his voice comes back, a miracle born of sin. When the pair head to New York together to restart his career the sex criminal socialite who violated the singer returns, so the prostitute kills him with a sword. Clearly Cain was trying to play around with and deflate some of the Hemingway masculinity that was plaguing literature after the birth of modernism. But there was no chance a film made in 1956 in America was going to feature *any* of that shit (but hey it does have blackface! Nothing wrong with that in 1956!), so when the 1937 novel was bought in 1944, it underwent a battery of rewrites and a series of potential directors, including Michael Curtiz, who, we must admit, would have made roughly the same movie. He *did* make an Elvis film. There's some dynamic framing and blocking (a scene with Joan Fontaine on the phone feels completely useless until J. Peverell Marley's camera follows her to her vanity mirror and Lanza storms in the door in its reflection; pretty slick) and bursts of color to heighten our understanding of the hero's psychological state. The stage shows, at their best, recall the wonders Mann worked while employed by W. Lee Wilder on *The Great Flamarion*.

Lanza's not a *terrible* actor, though he can't walk convincingly That is a problem. He *is* overly mannered, blinking and twitching and shaking as if he's worried he isn't presenting as human enough. This would have worked a little better in a film noir that remembered to behave like one, if they'd given his character a drug problem or made his trauma text instead of *very* deeply buried subtext. He would have made a fine enough character actor in crime films (he could have played a few of the parts in Huston's *Asphalt Jungle,* I feel), but no one used to the limelight will just give it up. Mann surrounded him with ringers. Vince Edwards is a passionate boxer, the same year as his role as Marie Windsor's no-good boyfriend in *The Killing*. Vincent Price is our gay impresario (who does *not* rape our hero) and Joan Fontaine his cocktail happy acquaintance with designs on Lanza; they've swapped genders for the sake of an American audience's sensibilities. Sara Montiel, a Spanish beauty who'd been under contract in Mexico and had lately made her American debut in Robert Aldrich's rollicking *Vera Cruz,* is the young woman who must gift Lanza his voice again. She would become Mrs. Mann for a few years after he and his camera fully drank her in. Harry Bellaver and his fifty acres of face play Lanza's manager. Joseph Calleia, two years before appearing in *Touch of Evil,* four before retiring, plays the great musician whom our hero idolizes. Mann admitted he was the wrong guy for this job, that the film probably shouldn't have been made, but he was glad to have worked with Lanza. Sometimes people come into your life for a brief moment, make a good, lasting impression, and leave, just like Peter Price all those years ago. Sometimes that's enough. Someone ought to remake this. Lots of insane ideas come and go between the arias.

Men in War – 1957

Korean War movies started before the war was over, but the tenor was different, the bloom off the rose before it had a chance to start dropping petals. World War 2 veteran and firebrand journalist Sam Fuller, only a few pictures deep into his illustrious career behind the camera, set the tone with *The*

Steel Helmet and *Fixed Bayonets!,* fatalist and unheroic, dirty and messy. The war itself would prove to be much the same, not least because when we lost, it became clear that we lost for a cause that was entirely fabricated to keep Douglas MacArthur's heart rate up so he could attempt to take over America by fiat. North Korea was never a threat, though many Americans still think they were. A man came up to me at a talk at Bryant Park where I was discussing John Ford and said of course he was *grateful* that we'd stopped North Korea invading the south but at what cost? I hadn't the heart to tell him the cost was him believing North Korea was going to invade South Korea. Nobody's immune to propaganda, least of all those who want to believe it. Unsurprisingly this *extremely* low budget film was nothing a major studio wanted to finance and Mann put up the money himself. To make it after three films about the most harmless kitschy middlebrow fixations of the 1950s (Mario Lanza, Glenn Miller, and great big beautiful airplanes flown by over the hill baseball players) was the ultimate reset. Mann was *alive* back there.

Men In War had to have been the only American war film to date that opens with orchestral stings right out of Stravinsky's *Rite of Spring.* Identical ghostly, stern faces stare out from darkness, as the credits smack the screen and Elmer Bernstein's music prepares for the worst. It's like a horror movie, or something by Kurosawa. Then a beautiful dolly shot through a smoldering hill past tired soldiers sitting like children in timeout. This war has already done a number on these poor bastards. But wait there's more! This was Mann's penultimate noir, making a horrible, frustrating ecosystem of paranoia and misery with close-ups and a philosophy of withholding images and information. When we happen upon Robert Ryan, the great eager dog of the Bs becomes the hard sleepless A-picture owl before our eyes, waiting for everybody, himself first, to die. Mann, like Welles, paved the way for the next decade of American cinema with his roving camera and itchy mise en scène. Stanley Kubrick had had this idea first with *Fear and Desire* he just didn't know what to do with it. He knew cinema needed to be reborn. Mann was just in the right place and the right time to do it. Not that anyone noticed...

The central conflict is between Ryan and Aldo Ray. Ryan just wants to live to see next week. Ray is obsessed with carrying out the mission of his catatonic commanding officer Robert Keith, who he is all but dragging through the front lines a la *Weekend at Bernie's*. The two *loathe* each other, a replay of the dichotomous conflict at the heart of so many Mann movies (*Last Frontier, Black Book, The Tall Target, The Man from Laramie, The Naked Spur*), the split in the soul between survival and honor (or nature and grace, as Malick would have it 55 years later). Ray can think of nothing more important than the man who can only become conscious long enough to smoke a cigarette. Ryan rips the blanket off Keith's lap and finds that Ray's tied him down to the jeep. "What the hell's this?!" Ryan asks as if it isn't and has never been the 1950s. Staring into its deep canyons and the pocked close-ups of faces that really appear to have seen into eternity you see more than the few Bronson Canyon vistas selected to stand in for Korea. Don Siegel would attempt this same feat in *Hell is for*

Heroes but you can't do this twice. Mann is at his inventive, despairing best here, the last of his low budget wonders.

The braindead colonel is our MacArthur stand-in, slowly losing it as he attempts to commit more and more troops to the field, his disgraceful genocidal attitude and meaningless war record all the encouragement a man like Ray (sort of a Curtis LeMay stand-in like Frank Lovejoy in *Strategic Air Command*) needs to keep following him. The most tender moment in the movie comes a full hour into rendering Ray as a stone faced and single-minded psychopath who would kill every Korean and American if it meant doing right by the shadow of the man he carries with him. Out of nowhere he's a few inches from Keith saying he misses when the man called him "son... you're the only man ever called me that." And this bloviating hulk suddenly seems like a little kid. A miracle of a performance, reading familial love and possibly more into the unchanging and unappealing face of Keith, a human Kuleshov effect, who can only make the occasional noise and swallow. And then, and stop reading here if you've never had the pleasure of watching this marvel, just when we're all but used to that the man lifts a finger to take the cigarette out of his mouth and a tantalizing possibility rears its head: he's been faking it to get back home after all his men and dozens more besides have died. But then something else: he rallies. And runs into battle to get shot and killed. *This* is the insanity of war, the everyday problem of the foot soldier that the film seeks to dramatize. Mann had helped change the western and the noir, then sent himself back to basic training and came out with a new kind of war picture, unsparing, unyielding, with a thinning unit and barely a hero in sight. Robert Aldrich, Sam Peckinpah, and Jean-Luc Godard were paying attention, even if no one else was.

The Tin Star – 1957

Henry Fonda isn't even half wanted in the little town he rides into with an outlaw's carcass slung over his pack horse. Not by sheriff Anthony Perkins, his girlfriend Mary Webster, dead man's brother and stable owner Neville Brand, doctor John McIntire, not mayor Howard Petrie, not brothers Lee Van Cleef and Peter Baldwin, not nobody. The only sympathetic ears in town belong to Michel Ray, the half-native son of widow Betsy Palmer (many years before her more famous son slaughtered all those kids at Camp Crystal Lake on a night just like tonight...). As badly as everyone wants him out of town though, incidents keep conspiring to waylay him. He's already been a sheriff once, maybe he ought to stick around and relieve Perkins of the job before some of the town's more trigger-happy elements puts him in a pine box and makes one more widow of the public.

The Tin Star, unsurprisingly, was supposed to be the ninth film Mann made with Jimmy Stewart, you can see the character of Morgan Hickman shaped and fitted for him like a pair of chaps and a Stetson. Fonda handles it beautifully, of course, no question he would have. He confesses that a shot that saved Perkins in a gunfight could just as easily have killed him and the two actors have to take in the news

200

together; wonderful two-part harmony. William Perlberg and George Seaton were star producers/directors blazing a trail across Hollywood after the former came up as Columbia founder Harry Cohn's assistant. They rode Mann too hard, believing themselves his equal artistically, which is a hilarious thing to believe of the man who just turned in *Men in War*. Seaton wasn't an incompetent, he made the very good *36 Hours* and about twenty other movies I never saw, but he did make *Airport,* so I'm afraid he's disqualified from the pantheon. Mann blamed them for the film's lack of purpose, and you can feel the hand of a liberal producer at work between the lugubrious pace and the message of acceptance. At 1.5 speed this might have approached a classic Mann western.

Loyal Griggs shot it on VistaVision and at times it feels like a TV movie (indeed like one of Don Siegel's, who played with these themes himself in *Death of a Gunfighter* and *Stranger on the Run*), what with the handsome deep-set lines, the functional indoor compositions, and the obvious soundstage recorded dialogue and the even more obvious Elmer Bernstein score (a lot of late 50s black and white westerns all had this problem). Not shocking to learn Seaton and Perlberg worked with Robert Mulligan, this is exactly the kind of movie he would have made. The film resists complicating its plot at every turn, disappointingly. There are chances to implicate or indict Fonda in the crimes that beguile the evil little town, there's even a hint that they might kill a cute kid, and at every turn the easy solution is found and then chosen. Perkins and Fonda start as enemies, slowly become reluctant allies, and then finally stand together against a posse stoked by Brand's hatred of Native Americans. The elements are here, the fire is gone. The best moments are visual, but they're few and far between. Fonda and Perkins wait in the locked jailhouse for the posse to attack, and then they throw a rock through the window finally, the blinds come up and there they sit, all 50 of them. Really stark and frightening, as are the conflicting images of Perkins staring them down. At last Mann seems in his element bridging an impossible gap of 20 feet and all the civilization contained in each step. A fine close to a missed opportunity.

God's Little Acre – 1958

Erskine Caldwell's been pretty well
forgotten since his heyday in the 1930s
writing one popular Hillbilly drama or
comedy after another. John Ford's worst
regarded film was an adaptation of the play
based on his *Tobacco Road*, which ran
forever and a day on the great white way.
God's Little Acre was also a blockbuster
book, so much so the film adaptation opens
by calling it the best-selling book of all time
(the lady doth protest, etc.) before filling our
ears with the braying of cobwebbed hillbilly
humor. Robert Ryan lusts after his
daughter-in-law, Buddy Hackett shows up,
there's talk of albino's being scientifically
able to see through solid dirt, like the one
they've got tied up in the barn. It's not a
promising start. Blacklisted Ben Maddow
claimed he wrote the script instead of
credited Philip Yordan, though why he'd
want credit for this I'm not so sure. There is
something to the idea of Caldwell's works
creating the space for Tennessee Williams
and William Inge's much better but still

sensational works about the Deep South to reshape the American theater (though by now William Faulkner's tales of deformed gothic grace had plowed those fields, too, as well as films like Jean Renoir's *Swamp Water*, Borzage's *Moonrise* or Andre De Toth's *Dark Water*) but that doesn't make them that much easier to sit through. The book was censured for obscenity, and you can see Williams' and Elia Kazan's *Baby Doll* having sprung from its well, though both play and movie beat this film to the punch, making it look all the more cartoonish in its wake.

The plot is simple, if discursive. Ryan believes his grandfather buried gold under his property a hundred years ago and has spent 15 years searching for it. One of those conceits you only ever find in literature and theatre; very cute and tidy metaphors. He's warped sons Vic Morrow, Jack Lord, and Lance Fuller, daughters Fay Spain and Helen Westcott with his single-minded quest for gold, and life has sorta passed them by in the meantime. Westcott's husband Aldo Ray (just beautiful, can't take your eyes off of him) is trying to get the local mill opened up. If the book was unpopular with Catholics for its depictions of sexuality, the film was also a scandal because of the subplot involving Ray whipping up an insurrection among laid off workers who want to seize the means of production from bosses. For every hoary dipshit cliche about the south, there are grace notes like this or Rex Ingram's performance as Ryan's head sharecropper. Mann and Maddow were both radicals in their way (the blacklist was a stupid criminal witch-hunt, but you could trust it to tell you which artists actually gave a shit about their fellow man). Mann was worried about the film being too theatrical, and so he and Ernest Haller (who, having shot a lot of *Gone with the Wind*, knew a thing or two about framing Southern indecorousness) gave it a stark monochromatic look and made sure the camera tripped drunkenly across its bleak landscapes. At times this is a really lovely work. They are short times.

The real subject is infidelity, with Ryan having obviously been betrayed by his grandfather, and Ray betrayed by the bosses at the mill, but of course every character here is leering and thinking unchristian thoughts. Ray is married to

Westcott, but lusts after Tina Louise, who's married to Lord, though Ryan also wants to screw Westcott, and Spain beds their pet albino, played by Michael Landon (yes, this makes this film is pre-*Bonanza* canon). Fuller, who also plays Brack in *This Island Earth* and worked for Ed Wood, got out of the house and married rich but his wife died and now he wants nothing to do with the family (we meet him in a robe, daintily chomping a cigar, having fully left behind his masculine hillbilly coding). There's incest around every corner though Mann never peers around enough to see it. The climax forgets most of this for the spectacle of Ray getting drunk and deciding tonight's the night. He's going to seduce Louise and turn the power back on in the valley while hundreds watch him. This is a better move than continuing to film the quest for Curly's Gold, but it makes you wonder what the first act and a half of the film was for. The security guard who shoots him screams over the sound of the machines that he needed the job desperately and didn't mean to do it. Capitalism as cannibalism. You can see everything from *Lolly Madonna XXX, Fat City, Norma Rae, The Molly Maguires, Slap Shot, Silkwood,* and *Swing Shift* emerging from under its apron. Ryan's penultimate scene is devastating and desperate. The movie becomes something shocking with its last fumes.

Man of the West – 1958

Man of the West is a perfect double entendre. Indeed Robin Wood made it explicit in his marvelous essay on the director's sojourns to the dusty trail end, "Man(n) of the West". It was his last film of the 50s, the conclusive end of his days as a director of American genre before becoming an ill-fated maker of epics, a film as big as it is compact. Wood called it the finest cinemascope film of the 50s (and, marvelously, said it paved the way for *The Hills Have Eyes* and *The Texas Chain Saw Massacre*), and it is by any measure one of the best westerns of its golden age, which makes it one of the finest films ever made. The 1950s American western gave us *The Searchers, Wagon Master, Ride Lonesome, Johnny Guitar, Day of the Outlaw, Forty Guns, Apache Drums,*

Westbound, Seminole, Terror in a Texas Town to say nothing of Mann's own *The Naked Spur, The Furies, Winchester '73,* and *The Man from Laramie,* and still *Man of the West* stands tall. Gary Cooper began the decade in the divisive (and we must admit inferior) *High Noon* as a hero without a friend and ended it as a villain who lives long enough to reform. *Man of the West* is about changing, but also about knowing who you are. In short it's the ideal Mann film, and not surprisingly it wasn't a hit in America. Godard loved it, comparing Mann to Matisse. He knew a little something about reinvention, too.

Gary Cooper is Link Jones, former hood, now an upstanding member of the community of Little Hope sent to the city to look for a schoolteacher to bring back and help the place thrive. He boards the wrong train and when it gets held up by a gang (Jack Lord, J. Williams, Royal Dano, Robert J. Wilke) he and fellow passengers Julie London and Arthur O'Connell are left behind. London is a saloon singer, but O'Connell wants Cooper to hire her to be his schoolteacher. Maybe she can reform as he has? Cooper knows the cabin they happen upon when they start walking for help. It belonged to a man he once knew, and he doesn't just mean himself. His uncle (Lee J. Cobb) is in there along with the three train robbers, and he was the man who trained Link to be a killer and also the last man Link tried to kill before going legit. He lies and says London is his girl hoping it'll keep the outlaws from pawing her too much. It doesn't work and after Williams is sacrificed to prove this gang won't hesitate to kill anybody, they turn on London and Cooper, demanding she undress in front of them and she gets mighty close for 1958, while Cooper bleeds and sweats under Lord's knife. Would it shock you to learn the Catholic League of Decency condemned the film?

Stories differ on this but apparently Jimmy Stewart wanted the part of Link pretty badly but Mann wouldn't consider him. They'd parted ways after disagreeing over the direction of the movie *Night Passage* (supposedly Mann felt Stewart just wanted to make that very boring movie because it allowed him the chance to play the accordion) which James Neilson ended up directing and I'm guessing you haven't heard of it either. I sure hadn't. Like James Whitmore and Victor Mature the ages of Cooper and Cobb should have been reversed for the story to work but of course no one played an ornery old son of a bitch like Cobb, who had just been in another Reginald Rose scripted drama of moral equivocation: *12 Angry Men*. Cooper hadn't done a western since *Vera Cruz in 1954,* and if he's too old to play Link Jones he makes more sense than he did romancing Audrey Hepburn in the dreary *Love in the Afternoon* the year prior. Mann was beleaguered by Rose's demands as the writer and the producers' unwillingness to budge, but he managed to instill in the film a kind of moral frustration that keeps it fascinating. It's another of Mann's Shakespearean westerns, with allegiances shifted and masks donned to fool small clans from the hero's true intentions. We know what Cooper is and what he's pretending to be, but we don't know what he'll do when pushed back into his old life.

Ernest Haller returned after *God's Little Acre* to shoot this gorgeous group of landscapes and the miserable pirates who crawl through it to their next act of violence.

He uses distance in the frame exquisitely, like he's writing in cursive, staging little dramas and confabs at different ends of the screen, across the X, Y, and Z axes. Lord and Cooper have a messy, knockdown drag out brawl all across the frame (at one point Lord almost *jumps with both feet* on Cooper's chest) to show there's nowhere you can run or hide from the violence and then Cooper starts *taking Lord's clothes off* to humiliate him as repayment for what he did to London the night before. She isn't sure what to make of that, but we in the audience hearing his wailing and crying sure are. Like the Budd Boetticher and Randolph Scott movies it was released alongside (which were getting better as they went), *Man of the West* concerns a few people who learn the depths to which they're willing to sink to make a point about dignity and accountability. They ride into a ghost town in the final act, a place where civilization failed out of existence and only the shells of buildings and what they represent remain (their abandoned fences like bones distancing the desperadoes in the final shootout, further enunciating the widescreen choreography of the camera). Cooper tries to purge himself of his worst urges to avoid becoming just like it; a living warning, a human skeleton. That's harder than you think when without money you have no reputation (even a man trying to hire a schoolteacher knows this). A man walks into the desert to prove he's not nothing. He must become less than that before he returns. All of civilization a put-on, a costume, a choice.

Cimarron – 1960

1960 was a bad year for Anthony Mann. He quit Spartacus due to trouble with star Kirk Douglas (though they buried the hatchet in 1965 in order to make *The Heroes of Telemark, to neither of their benefit*) and then quit *Cimarron* with something like half the production schedule left to the fulfilled, which director and former choreographer Charles Walters did for them, uncredited. After having reshot some of *Gigi* when Vincente Minelli was away, he was already on MGM's list of pinch hitters and stepped in and finished the rest. The project was already compromised when he showed up.

Mann wanted to film on location but storms and floods made the executives nervous, so they rebuilt the set inside. Mann wanted a darker ending and even shot it, but they changed it in the editing room. Furthermore, the idea was a bad one and the kind of marketing logic that led studios to nearly go bankrupt in the late 60s. Richard Fleischer would fall prey to it with *Doctor Dolittle, Joseph Mankiewicz* with *Cleopatra,* George Stevens with *The Greatest Story Ever Told,* Lewis Milestone with *Mutiny on the Bounty,* etc. They thought that bigger movies would get people out of their houses and away from their televisions. MGM had already made *Raintree County* on 65mm, a film now best known as the one where Montgomery Clift almost died in a car crash while he was making it. He was at a party at Liz Taylor's house and crashed his roadster and as Kevin McCarthy called the police, Liz pulled his teeth out of his throat to stop him from tearing his own esophagus apart. The film continued shooting after Clift had had cosmetic surgery and his face is buried under makeup for half the film to hide the fact. *Raintree County* was otherwise a completely undistinguished movie that no one much cared for and still don't. This still left rival studios' elephantine westerns like *Giant* and *The Big Country to inspire them to make more of the same.* With the receipts for those sitting like a Dear John letter on the end table MGM decided another 65mm epic was what America needed and so immediately put one into production and then started sabotaging it at every turn. Was it a hit? Brother, it wasn't even shot on 65mm.

Still Mann at least got to hire some of his guys to come out and make it. Mann vets Arthur O'Connell, Royal Dano, L.Q. Jones, Harry (Henry) Morgan, Vic Morrow, Charles McGraw, Edgar Buchanan, and Robert Keith provided support for leads Glenn Ford and Maria Schell (playing a settler named Sabra...), who had a disastrous affair on the set. Also here somewhere was a jobbing character actor by the name of Coleman Francis, who later became a director himself. Anyone who knows me knows how exciting I find that. So if we consider that Mann had his work chopped up in post by executives, he loathed the studio shoot, he was replaced at the eleventh hour, and half the dialogue is *rampant* ADR, just what are we to judge *his* in this film. Besides some handsome set-ups, this is a deeply uneven and slow-moving epic (not unlike *Raintree County* and the later *The Four Horsemen of the Apocalypse,* which all but killed Ford's career) with unusual politics. When Russ Tamblyn, George Brenlin, and Vic Morrow ride up to try and...I don't know exactly, rape Maria Schell? It's unclear... Glenn Ford shoots at them but then realizes they're old friends of his and lets them go. And that's how the movie *starts.*

Cimarron is about the Oklahoma Land Rush but is mostly an excuse to get a thousand extras in wagons on screen (which the bigwigs at MGM didn't even really want). And, my love for *the Lord of the Rings* movies notwithstanding, you can really only point your camera at a big crowd so many times and expect the audience to gasp in awe. And in order for the scope to continue to drive the piece you've got to constantly be talking about the land and the promise of a brighter future and the beautiful country it's going to build. Some writers are better than others about this... The flow of the piece is a *mess*. Glenn Ford exits the film for twenty minutes for no

215

reason and comes back a veteran of San Juan Hill. What?

The real interest in films like this is in the relationships. Glenn Ford has to explain his new marriage to old flame Anne Baxter, who, intriguingly threatens to shoot Ford dead when they reunite. She's more of a sexual threat than Schell, especially once her hatred cools, but Ford, ever the boy scout, won't ever leave his wife for her. Ford is consistently on the right side of history (he's opposed to the economic reforms and conditions that lead directly to the events of the movie *Killers of the Flower Moon,* in an interesting twist) but rarely interesting to watch. There are great camera movements, close-ups and blocking during these sequences, but those are few and far between, and the enormity of everything means very few intimate beats (Glenn Ford stroking dead Russ Tamblyn's hair, his reunion with Schell after a prolonged absence) really register, dwarfed as they are by scale and a desire to lurch to the end credits. Oil strikes, race riots, land rushes, marriage, death, birth; this movie has everything. And that's the problem.

El Cid – 1961

Mann and Philip Yordan's respective radical streaks did have a ceiling. He wasn't a vocal Hollywood liberal like, say, John Huston or Kirk Douglas, and then when push came to shove, he got into bed with the fascists, if indirectly. Producer Samuel Bronston had opened a studio in Spain with the express purpose of doing business with Francisco Franco. When the Generalissimo found out Bronston wanted to make a film of the life of Castilian warlord Rodrigo Díaz de Vivar, dubbed El Cid, he was thrilled. You see the Generalissimo always *identified with* El Cid, and he would just love to see himself up there on the big screen, if you please. And whatever estimation I hold Mann and Yordan in, they gave the general just what he wanted. This was the age of the epics, as short lived as it is titanic and monolithic, still casting a shadow over American cinema today. As entertaining as they could be, they were never as good as they could be, and frankly the batting average of this 3-hour

217

clodhopper is like Bill Bergen's. Mann managed to hire as many people of their characters' actual ethnicity as David Lean managed in the better regarded and just plain better *Lawrence of Arabia* but he couldn't manage as many minutes of cinema per hour. It was nearly a fifth over before I saw a single shot I found compelling, a split diopter across the Super-Technirama 70mm frame, which is cheating.

El Cid has scarcely begun when the problems start. Within minutes we're watching crowds of people having discussions of policy and battle plans in front of hundreds of extras as the camera just sort of stands there like one of them. Robert Krasker, who shot *The Third Man,* was the director of photography, too, so there's *really* no excuse between him and Mann for the flat staging and frequent cutting. Even John Ford let him do his Dutch tilts, completely out of character. Charlton Heston is riding to his wedding to Sophia Loren (to secure her participation two additional screenwriters were hired to flesh out her character) when he happens upon a sacked village and decides to free some Muslim prisoners of war (led by super soul brothers Douglas Wilmer and Frank Thring), binding them together. They dub him Al Sidi, which becomes El Cid in Spanish. In so doing he becomes an enemy of the Spanish crown. Like Mann's heroes in *Cimarron, The Tin Star, The Last Frontier, etc,* Heston's sympathy and empathy mark him as an outcast in a bloodthirsty society. What choice does he have but to conquer it, to make his own success?

Mann seems seduced by the enormity and import of all things, perhaps because he'd seen what a successful epic looked like (he worked on *Quo Vadis* for a few days and fled *Spartacus* with a headache, and now he was finally getting to do the thing for himself). Thus I can find no real excuse for a three hour movie to have 30 minutes of real moviemaking. Dull conversations are shot in dull mediums, crowd scenes take in the geometrically pleasing shapes that surround them, sword fights are rendered limp by the edit. You could cut all of this together compellingly but everything just sits there. He wakes up a little by the end of the first hour with a jousting match and an awards ceremony where Heston gets his first commission. Even perennially out of touch Bosley Crowther called this out and yes, it's "impressive", but no other aspect of the production buoys it under all that heavy gold plating, so sink it must. A beautifully weird goth symmetrical funeral parade is interrupted by snapping and knife fighting by actors (Gary Raymond and John Fraser) who have not calibrated to the tone of the movie - it's more than *El Cid* can take, a sudden outbreak of *Lion in Winter* by way of Robert Fuest or Michael Carreras.

And yet all this movie can't help but have influenced *someone*. Ridley Scott's *Kingdom of Heaven* at times feels like a direct remake, Peter Jackson was reaching for it in *The Lord of the Rings,* and Martin Scorsese *loved it,* supervising its comprehensive restoration in the 90s. I guess every kid who saw it when they were young was duly impressed by the size and longed to have some of it for themselves. Heston's gravitas is always kind of persuasive, but he does slow the movie down to his steady robotic heartbeat, not yet let off the chain by Sam Peckinpah and *Planet of the Apes*. The sound of him saying "You'll make a Muslim of me yet," is the kind of kitschy insanity you expect from the middlebrow Mann's by now. He gets much heft when called upon to swear on a bible; he's much less attuned to confessions of love. It doesn't help that he's once more playing Ben Hur, a Christ figure who can do no wrong, even killing for the right reasons. He backs out of a plot to help protect a prince only to be bummed when the prince takes matters into his own hands and kills someone to stay alive. How's the moral high ground up there, Cid? Air nicer?

A narrator occasionally leaps in to tell us what's happening - never a good sign. I checked my phone. Often. If every scene were as good as its best and every shot as interesting, the three hours would have passed like an hour with an old friend. Mann huffs and puffs to build to *El Cid's* most awe-inspiring components. There are flourishes that remind of his histories, with their close-up consternation as the tides of history smash against locked doors; his westerns, with their glorious vistas dotted by horseback riders heading towards destiny; his noirs and musicals, with their grinding gears and outcast lovers shot with room for physicality. But a three-hour Anthony Mann epic really ought to feel more like one, and less like what it is: something he mounted and did his best to tame, but fell off a time or two too many, his weary bones not up to the task. Still I can't help but like these unwieldy Mann misfires. A guy who started out making *Dr. Broadway* ending his career commanding armies of Muslim horsemen and Spanish stuntmen while a dictator waited for the rushes is just too strange a story not to become invested. Only the movies made it possible. No one would get this worked up for a written biography or a song, would they?

The Fall of the Roman Empire – 1964

"My lord Caesar...the omens are bad..." It shocked no one, is my guess, when Samuel Bronston filed chapter 11 in 1964 right as he was planning to release his two biggest films to date: the completely forgotten and made-up sounding *Circus World* with John Wayne, (I'm not sure I have it in me to watch it and find out if it is indeed real), and his second collaboration with Anthony Mann, *The Fall of The Roman Empire, all three written by Philip Yordan*. I don't want to say it's a bad sign when you've researched a movie so thoroughly that before you've written page one of the script you have a 350-page document with facts and dates, and then the film begins with a conversation held halfway up a staircase, with neither character in focus, reams of exposition cascading into the ether. I knew I was in trouble. Stanley Kubrick researched Napoleon so heavily he was meant to have a room with card catalogues so meticulously filed that he could open it and tell you to the minute what the man was up to on what day of his life, and that movie never got made. A case could be made that Anthony Mann would have been better off if he'd never stopped researching this one. At times it feels like it's still being made, the reels being loaded into your copy while it drags on and on, kinda like the end of Kiss' "Black Diamond." They say on cold, lonely nights you can still hear "Black Diamond" refusing to fucking end.

So what on earth is *The Fall of the Roman Empire* about, minute to minute? An empire can't fall every act, can it? Well fans of demonstration are sure in luck because nary a character enters the story without the wave of an arm and a vocal description. "ah yes...Caesar's daughter!" People can complain all they want about *Gladiator,* and I'll be first in line, but Ridley Scott found a way to make the thing move at least. After Tucker Johnson and I finished *The End of History* we went and celebrated with a screening of *Gladiator* on 35mm at the Somerville Theater and the man introducing it (amazing they bothered hiring one for one of the most popular films of the last 30 years) planted a quote in our brains we'll never forget. "Ridley Scott boarded the project and hired many historians to help him achieve a depth of detail and a real feeling for life in the Roman Empire. Within a couple of weeks it became clear that Scott himself actually didn't *care* how accurate he was being, and the film he was planning was pure Hollywood fantasy. The historians… *quit.*" I want it on a t-shirt. "The Historians Quit," maybe in Papyrus font. Well when they don't quit you get this parade of faces and names that never come into focus except when you recognize the actor playing him. You know...history.

A lot of people were asked to play Livius the lead, but I think they realized which way the wind was blowing. That Stephen Boyd ended up with it and he's still only thought of as the guy in *Ben Hur* who isn't Ben Hur is explanation enough why a bigger name or more talented thespian didn't pursue the part. Boyd is only *this much more* acceptable than Robert Taylor in *Quo Vadis* and looks like Brian Thompson or some other bodybuilding bit playing tough, uncomfortable face mashed into a helmet like too much crust over a pie tin, and he projects nothing like the grandiosity you'd need to keep this from drying up. Richard Harris turned the part down and wound up playing Caesar anyway when Scott came calling with his remake at the end of the century. The usual suspects round out the cast: Alec Guinness as Marcus Aurelius, Sophia Loren as his daughter, James Mason back from Mankiewicz' superior *Julius Caesar,* Christopher Plummer, Mel Ferrer, Omar Sharif ported over from David Lean's camp, Anthony Quayle, John Ireland, who was sort of Stephen Boyd.0, and the always-welcome Andrew Keir, the best Professor Quatermass. With so much emphasis on great and theoretically great actors gravely intoning platitudes on huge sound stages or out in enormous landscapes in front of a trillion extras I forgot anyone was directing this thing, let alone the man who made *The Tall Target*. It seems impossible to imagine anyone thought this would do anything *but* bankrupt its producer.

Mann's direction is sluggish in the utmost. Though of course he died making it, it was still heartening to see Mann close his career with a film noir because at least Christopher Challis knew how to move the camera around those cramped, ugly spaces like John Alton once did. He was likely just happy he wasn't lugging a VistaVision mount up a Greek mountain in half-darkness like he did for Michael Powell on *Ill Met By Moonlight*. Robert Krasker returns here from *El Cid* and though there's the occasional sweeping dolly or pan, mostly one gets the sense of the weight of every set up exceeding the heaving strength of his gaffers. Dimitri Tiomkin produced 150 minutes of music for this thing, some new breathless theme for everything from Stephen Boyd and Christopher Plummer holding hands to Stephen Boyd and Christopher Plummer drinking. It's less forceful than Miklós Rózsa's work on *El Cid* but maybe more lush? Tough to compare them, honestly, except to say there isn't a hook to be found in either score. Just pounds of music applied like pancake makeup on the face of a white British actor playing a Muslim. Little wonder everyone still plays some variation on Maurice Jarre's *Lawrence* music whenever their characters hit the sand and no one quotes this at gunpoint.

It was about an hour of great thudding nothing before something of interest finally happened. James Mason is trying to reason with king of the German barbarians (John Ireland. Who were you expecting?) and they grab him and torture him. Panic in his eyes, he tells them he's not afraid of what they'll do to them but that if he screams the romans will come in and slaughter them all. Mason withstands the torture, earns their respect and he immediately despairs. This noble enemy just ditched their god because a poet could hold up under enhanced interrogation? What a disappointment! But he quickly rallies and takes them for allies anyway. Five-minute essay on the plight of conqueror and conquered in the middle of all this pomp and parading, with James Mason as our guide to boot. Hilariously Mann stated his aim with this was to dramatize how eras end, governments and movements rise and fall. But the movie ends with a voiceover saying "ok yeah Rome didn't really fall here, but it did eventually!" You mean to tell me that I sat through three hours of lectures and the fucking thing didn't even *fall?!!?*

The Heroes of Telemark – 1965

Finally free of Samuel Bronston and his rolodex of fascists, Anthony Mann was in a place to do a little light reinvention. Trouble is he was an American in his 50s in the 60s, a bad time to be playing catch-up with the rest of the cinema. Even people who survived Arthur Penn's slate cleaning *Mickey One* and *Bonnie & Clyde,* like John

Huston and Richard Fleischer, didn't get there intact and Mann can't really be said to have made it at all. *The Heroes of Telemark,* his second World War 2 film, was a little lighter on its feet than his previous few films, but between the chintzy Malcolm Arnold score (like the theme from an Italian superhero film), lead duties split between Richard Harris and Kirk Douglas, old-school bad special effects, no model he was yet paying attention to (no Godard to teach him jump cuts, no Sembène to further empower his racial progressivism, no Resnais to tell him to play with time and dreams) and a big old cinemascope ratio to capture it all this was still one tired film. Not a single Mann player joined him in the mid 60s, though cinematographer Robert Krasker, his Dutch tilts having been hammered French by Mann and Bronston's awards bait, hung around, no good to anyone else now that he'd lost his signature style. Nobody was going for broke, except Mann, who had gambling debts to pay.

The Heroes of Telemark was made to cash in on the burgeoning market of Alistair MacLean adaptations after *The Guns of Navarone* and the first few James Bond movies had proved so successful (these films were counter programming to the kinds of movies Mann had spent the first half of the decade making). This even had its heroes skiing before Bond took it up on screen in *On Her Majesty's Secret Service* (a movie that is just as bad and boring as people said it was before revisionism rescued it from the rubbish heap, even graced by the presence of Diana Rigg, most beautiful woman on earth). But it was also based on true events and *two* (!) books. Harris leads a spy mission to the Vemork Norsk Hydro plant in Rjukan, Norway, in the county Telemark, which has a skiing maneuver named after it. He and Douglas, playing a *Norwegian physics professor* (!!!???) have to take evidence back to England of the plant's being used by Nazis to develop atomic weapons (they should have taken a longer trip to America so they could have called ahead and asked what office they wanted at NASA). Douglas mentions wanting to have his work checked by Einstein and Oppenheimer but the film doesn't seem interested in the ramifications of us bringing the same villains we were defeating to Fort Bliss. It's not like it was a secret, no matter what *For All*

Mankind would have you believe. By 1946 Wernher Von Braun's second-in-command Walther Reidel was already having magazine profiles written about adjusting to civilian life; evidently he didn't like the way Americans prepared chicken.

The whole thing is fair enough but Mann and Krasker and editor Bert Bates aren't really interested in making an action movie. Stuff rears its head, gets dealt with, end of scene. There's no urgency to the choreography or staging even when the actors are really going for it with the running and shooting and whatnot. Apparently, Harold Pinter did a pass on this? At one point a scientist pauses to hang his coat up in the middle of a sentence about mutually assured destruction, which feels kind of Pinter. Kirk Douglas's ex-wife (Ulla Jacobsen) kicks him out of bed during their commando raid, which is also pretty Pinter-esque. Ditto the bit where she chucklingly points out a cute bunny rabbit, which then hops into the underbrush and explodes. "Land mines," sighs Douglas. Oh and his cover is as a skiing tourist...in a town covered in landmines... it's at least shocking, even if it doesn't make any fucking sense. Then Anton Diffring's Nazi major checks in on them as they pretend to neck in a cabin like he's the peeved dean in a snobs v. slobs frat house comedy. Very weird.

Mann films the dripping doohickies in the hydro station with appropriate menace (and Krasker manages to re-inflate his Dutch tilt for a few seconds at a time) and you can feel him flexing to try and get his muscle memory to kick in (by *A Dandy in Aspic* it had but it was too late - he was dead before the wrap party, which must have been a pretty dreary affair). There are flashes of the old professionalism. Some blocking, a bit of camera calisthenics, the landscape as ever yawning behind our heroes, but it can't live up to its director's best work or indeed the films it's trying to best. Our heroes even sing a song like the POWs in *Bridge Over The River Kwai*. Mann finally fully seems in command of his senses when his commandos start their wordless raid on the plant. Everything vanishes and the sheer distance between objects finally impresses. Not even *Where Eagles Dare (more boring than you remember)* managed this. Neither did *Guns of Navarone,* come to think of it...

232

Douglas' casting finally makes sense, too. Not that he didn't make a credible... *quickly scanning document* Norwegian physics professor... but when lugeing towards the camera on a nocturnal attack, he fits like a glove. Harris is good all the way through, never overplaying his hand and, knowing he can't win the film away from Douglas, doesn't try. Smart. He broods, he snaps, he fades in and out of darkness. He would have made an ok Bond if he weren't so pale.

In one bit of the big set piece, two of the men go clip a lock off a gate. The noise is loud. They duck. Mann messes up by not showing us the relationship between the men on the ground and the sentries who come to check the noise. But he saves it. The camera waits as the two nazi guards shine their lights under their deck attached to the guard house, then walk into a door and go inside, then Mann dollies past the door to the edge of the deck to see the commandos continuing on their way, some 30 feet in the distance. Very sexy stuff. I submit there was no better approach to *that* shot, which isn't often a feeling one has in Mann after 1958. Our leads don't speak for something like 20 minutes right smack in the middle of the film like the heist in *Rififi,* and the Nazis only get in a few words in the margins, and they linger in their dumb randomness. "Hehllooo...helllooo...." says the man guarding the hydro plant workings, so loud, completely unaware he's about to lose his job and his life. It's the "what now?" and "why?" of the little details that make it work.

There are still problems, of course. You don't get to know anyone else in the nearly dozen-man team sent to blow up the plant. Missed opportunity in a two-and-a-half-hour movie, but hardly the only one, so perhaps a paltry complaint. David Cairns points out that Chris Nolan must have been a fan as he lifts big chunks of it for *Inception,* and without knowing this I compared the horrifying *Tenet* to *A Dandy in Aspic.* Mann talked about loving Murnau, which I'm sure raised a few eyebrows at the time but he got very close to the best of Murnau. Nolan has yet to touch the hem of Mann's trouser leg. Even a film as compromised and unsteady as *The Heroes of Telemark* is beautiful *and* suspenseful. Nolan hasn't quite managed either since *The Prestige*, which was almost 20 years ago.

A Dandy in Aspic – 1968

"A double agent hired to kill...*himself!*" promised the posters for this very queer capper to the career of the great Anthony Mann. I submit to you that those ellipsis don't really hide how funny that is as a tagline. "007, I need you to kill...*yourself!*" The film is basically in on the joke though the film always stops itself just in time from becoming an outright comedy. The mood is too grey. The paranoia a little too thick. Though *The Tall Target* was the official follow-up to *Reign of Terror* or *Black Book,* Mann's great period spy noir, *A Dandy in Aspic* has more of its DNA, with sniping functionaries and spooks running amok as Paris burns and each trying to use the apparatus of a new-and-yet-crumbling state to outwit the others. *Dandy,* based on a book by Derek Marlowe, finds Laurence Harvey as Eberlin, a British spy tasked with ferreting out and decommissioning a

Russian agent called Krasnevin. The trouble is he *is* Krasnevin and either did such a good job keeping it a secret his paymasters didn't realize it, or they did, and are messing with him before they bump him off. Either way, not an ideal position to be in, because one of you's bound to end up dead, and both of them are you. Shades of *Fight Club,* but, you know...better.

The book was much more abstract, with our hero Eberlin's state of mind a kind of labyrinth, where information and identity are pinged about like in the climax of *The Lady From Shanghai.* Mann wasn't interested in anything that existential and conceptual, having just fled lugubrious roadshow epics and in the mood for something *real.* But then he also probably wasn't expecting to have the heart attack that killed him 3/4 of the way through filming, just after the production had decamped to Berlin. Harvey finished directing the film, it got terrible reviews, and everyone agreed it best to let this one lie in the strange corner of damp English quasi-genre from which it had sprung along with Losey's *Secret Ceremony*, Jack Clayton's *Our Mother's House*, Jack Gold's *Retribution,* Peter

Collinson's *The Long Day's Dying,* Michael Reeves' *The Sorcerers,* and Tony Richardson's Jeanne Moreau diptych. It would most resemble Sidney Lumet's forgotten John Le Carré adaptation *Deadly Affair, the second George Smiley movie,* except Mann and Harvey's film has a sense of humor and pretensions towards mod styling, British New Wave grotesque immediacy, and post-Bond spectacle. And considering it's quite clearly being made with the Michael Caine Harry Palmer movies in mind (surprise hits that made Caine, who then dropped them to play the much less ambiguous and stunted Jack Carter), all of those competing influences have to do battle for the film's tone as if they were all in washing machine together. Add to that Anthony Mann in the director's chair, one time noir kingpin with no feel for modern politics, and things get even stranger.

Cinematographer Christopher Challis must have been invaluable help to Mann, having come of age shooting a handful of the most beautiful films ever made for Powell & Pressburger and also having grown up breathing in London's toxic atmosphere and watching her people slide into and out of wartime misery. The widescreen frame and the location shooting would have bonded Mann to Challis, and when they get arty with it, they both would have had about half of the puzzle in their heads. Busy apartments have frames upon frames waiting with each pan. Things look actually dark when they're meant to, a relief, and a must considering the subject matter and cold war atmosphere. The grotesque English and German settings seem borrowed from Antonioni, but then of course, as David Cairns *also* says Europe did just sort of look like this. See also: *The Living Dead at the Manchester Morgue* or *Tam Lin*. The split diopter is used much better here than it had been in Mann's previous work, as the film is all about splits and doubles and the things that can't be seen around corners and hiding in architectural tangles.

Marlowe's script is a hysterical thing, betraying his own book's subjectivity but finding brand new ways to make a spy caper unsexy. Open on a funeral, in which Harvey imagines the deceased tumbling from a high dive, muscles gleaming in the noonday sun (plainly the mission was in another country that day), and then the coffin lands with a thud in the match cut in the cold English mud. He shows up at a dinner club in a tuxedo like Bond but Elspeth March (who, herself, is sleeping with a twenty-year-old gigolo) coldly admonishes him. "He's absolutely sexless, abso*lutely* sexless, dear," she says to daughter Mia Farrow, who perks up like she's been told he's a millionaire with six weeks to live. Just what goes on in this reality?

Farrow was sort of already in such a situation, having just married Frank Sinatra and having been already driven half-mad by star makers in America. She looks at her skeletal figure in a mirror and concludes that she's "too voluptuous" for childbirth (?!??!!) before Harvey says something that works a little better on the page. "I'm always amazed that in this scientific age no one has yet perfected the art of making the common mirror. I haven't found one yet that has interpreted my image correctly." He's a vampiric figure, yes, but he's also not even really himself. In the mirror it sounds like something Derek Flint would say. Harvey accidentally lets himself into the bathroom on his way out of Mia Farrow's apartment. "There's no future in it," she giggles. And he looks around as if he'd lived his adolescence in it falling in love and muses "None at all." The idea of his having secret dalliances in men's rooms, and that being an integral part of spy craft, is brought up so much it's practically the point of the movie.

How did Mann decide this was going to be his next project? Had he always secretly longed to make more spy thrillers? Was he enticed especially to do so by producer Leslie Gilliat? Two things are basically certain: Gilliat hated shooting on location, and Mann was in debt. His old friend and collaborator John Alton ran into him in a Swiss casino during the production and as they planned to work together again (Alton had retired in 1960 so that would have been a real get) Alton couldn't help letting his eyes drift to the diminishing pile of chips in front of his pal. Mann couldn't stop now, even with Samuel Bronston's dirty money in his pocket. He had two ex-wives and one current wife to support. He's got something in common with his slippery hero. Eberlin pines to return to Russia, to drop his cover as a British spy and all the horrific things he has to pretend he isn't in the UK. Mann must have been a little confused about his own identity by now. Certainly the smile on Harvey's face when he meets old friend Per Oscarsson down by the docks, one of the few moments of genuine emotion he displays throughout, says that these men, director and star/director, were tired of their double lives. The ending, which Harvey shot, and is made...*touching* by his less than sure touch.... is the same as Monte Hellman's *The Shooting,* in which it's clear that someone is destroying Harvey, himself, or Tom Courtenay, who has throughout acted like his replacement and shadow, a different kind of double. But the threat is the same throughout: dissolving only to discover that beneath your skin the whole time there you were. No secret at all. Just a man, after all, and one who wasted his life. A fear, I feel, to which many people can relate.

A Dandy in Aspic wasn't meant to be his last film, of course, Harvey, also having a tough time coming up with his next act, finished it with Challis as his guide. The

Berlin-set finale cannot be said to be an accurate representation of what Mann would have done, but the idea of a film about a man with a split personality itself being caught between a dead man's wishes and a lost man's desperation is too perfect and too strange a coincidence for the film to do anything but gain eerie power. At the site of its stitches like Frankenstein's monster, personalities seeping out like oozing wounds going south.

Mann's compositions, the cattiness of the screenplay, and the constant sexualization of spy craft remind us of Mann's best films, which put a nation's ideals in the bodies of a few people in civilizations a hairsbreadth from collapse. You hear the echoes of their screams in the haunted corridors and alleys of *Aspic* as clearly as Harvey hears the accusations against him and his own guilt ringing out in his head. Mann had made what are still some of the best American movies and took to the novel's setting and grotesque textures like a fish to water, his cinemascope framing sharper than it had ever been. He may have become a director as lauded as his talents deserved had he lived. But now this nagging ear worm is his epitaph, half a film, half a statement, half a personality, half a life unlived. One film for a dozen broken promises. Perhaps the ultimate farewell. An artists last breath hidden somewhere between takes, as everywhere the cast thins, and countries, and their agents, crumble to dust. Disappeared. For good.

Printed in Great Britain
by Amazon